IMAGES
of England

LUDLOW
THE SECOND SELECTION

To "Lucky"
love
Happy
[signature]

This view of Ludlow was taken by Gareth Thomas from Titterstone Clee Hill using a telescopic lens. It shows the town clustered in the middle distance, with part of the buisness park on the left, and newly built houses along Parys Road to the right. Beyond are the wooded slopes of Whitcliffe and High Vinnals, with the Welsh hills in the far distance. The towers of the parish church and the castle rise above the town, beacons of Ludlow's historic importance.

IMAGES
of England

LUDLOW

THE SECOND SELECTION

Compiled by
David Lloyd and Gareth Thomas

TEMPUS

First published 2000
Copyright © David Lloyd and Gareth Thomas, 2000

Tempus Publishing Limited
The Mill, Brimscombe Port,
Stroud, Gloucestershire, GL5 2QG

ISBN 0 7524 2155 7

Typesetting and origination by
Tempus Publishing Limited
Printed in Great Britain by
Midway Clark Printing, Wiltshire

This book is dedicated to Daphne Jones and Jenny Vaughan,
tireless workers for many good causes in Ludlow, both of whom have greatly helped
in the production of this book.

The Horseshoe Weir, showing the Old Street mills on the left.

Contents

Acknowledgements

We are grateful to the following for the loan or donation of photographs and other materials, or for information received: Rick Alexander, Peter Bartlett, Graham Berlyn, the late John Berry, Pat Boreman, Ann Buckley, Hilary and Vince Bufton, Ena Burton, Charles Carter, Howard Cheese, Yvonne Cherry, John Coxall, Derek Davies, Jennifer Davies, the late Judy Deakin, Jennifer Donald, David Edwards, Linda Entecott, Lucy Eyelf, Daphne Farr, the late Connie Faulkner, David Faulkner, Ludlow Festival, Jack Gatehouse, Marie Glaze, Harvey Griffiths, Barbara Hall, Ronald Harris, Muriel Howard, Gwynn Howells, Janet George, Joyce Lilley, The Imperial War Museum, May Jackson, Lottie James, Chris Jeffery, Daphne Jones, Rosemary Jones, Gwendolen Llewellyn-Jones, Neville Jones, Shirley Lloyd, the late George Merchant, Marilyn Morris, Ludlow Museum, Ludlow Photographic Club, Ludlow Race Club, Ludlow Town Football Club, Ludlow Townswomen's Guild, Sylvia Martin, Keith Mellings, Jan Montieth, Bill Moody, John and Cheryl Needham, John Norton, The Old Ludlovians' Association, Denis Nash, Avril Norton, Helen Pearce, Pat Perry, Eileen Precious, Jenny Price, John Price, Phyllis Ray, Myra Reeves, Garth Reynolds, Bob and Jan Rose, Celia Rowlands, Ellis Shaw, Shropshire Records and Research, South Shropshire District Council, Harry Smith, Dick Stephens, Paul Suthern, the late Else Tilley, Charles Underhill, Jenny Vaughan, Ann Waite, the late David Williams, Sheila Williams, the late Connie Williams, Eric and Dereen Yeo. The photographs on pp 2, 93 (lower), 103, 112, 113, 114, 120, 121 (upper), 123 (upper), 124, 127 (lower) and 128 and the cover picture are by Gareth Thomas.

Introduction

This book is a successor to the first Ludlow volume in *The Archive Photographs* series, published in 1995. That book presented a collection of just over 200 pictures of 'Old Ludlow', compiled by David Lloyd with the assistance of other members of Ludlow Historical Research group. The photographs were arranged thematically into fourteen chapters, some of which covered geographical parts of the town, such as Corve Street, Linney and Galdeford, while others dealt with topics such as 'Earning a Living' and 'Wartime'.

The present volume is also a collection of Ludlow photographs, but the arrangement is different in two ways. Firstly, the book is the collaborative work of two people, David Lloyd and Gareth Thomas. David brings to the book his life-long interest in the history of the town and a host of personal memories going back to the late 1930s. He has written a number of books and articles on Ludlow, including *The Concise History of Ludlow*, published for the millennium in 1999. Gareth, a native of south-west Wales who settled in Ludlow in 1968, working first as a veterinary surgeon, then as a professional photographer, has brought to the book his own considerable knowledge of the town and district, together with his specialist photographic skills, including his developing interest in digital photography. Secondly, whereas the first volume spanned three centuries, with eight illustrations from before 1800, this one confines itself to the twentieth century, with a chapter for each decade. The twentieth century has been a time of cataclysmic change, with astonishing human achievements alongside times of terror and anguish. In 1911 a postcard from a young Ludlovian, Harry Roberts, starting a farm in the upper Murray valley in South Australia, took three months to reach relatives in Ludlow. By contrast in 2000 another former Ludlow Grammar School boy, Trevor Hoskins, living in Port Ludlow in the north-west of the United States, was able to order an advance copy of this book by e-mail. In this century, nearly two hundred young men from Ludlow died in the two world wars. Their names are recorded in the porch of St Laurence's parish church, and their memories are kept prominently in the public eye by the fine memorial in Castle Square dedicated to their memory in September 2000.

This book seeks to show how the events of this tumultuous century have impacted on Ludlow. Even at the start of the century Ludlovians were reminded that they were part of the wider world, as in an advertisement in *The Ludlow Advertiser*, 10 December 1920, which began

'T. and E. Bradley
16 King Street,
who have faithfully represented your wants in the Ludlow
Portion of His Majesty's Empire for over 20 years.'

Ludlow is no longer a portion of a world wide empire, but it still responds to events far beyond its boundaries, as many of the items in this book make clear.

Although two names only appear on the title page, this book, like its pedecessor, is essentially a commnity venture. Both authors are well-known as lecturers, and have given many illustrated talks on aspects of Ludlow and its countryside. This has led to the loan or gift of other photographs and has enabled many of the people on the photographs to be identified. This kind of interest in 'Old Ludlow', which comes from all sections of the community, but especially from families established here for generations, is infectious, and there have been many talks specifically on this topic, including the annual afternoon for Ludlow's senior citizens, provided by the Town Council. The authors are glad to acknowledge the help that they have had from many people, both at formal occasions, such as these, and also from people met casually in the streets of Ludlow.

Against this general background, this book has arisen from an exhibition in the 2000 Ludlow Festival called: *Twentieth Century Ludlow. a Pictorial Journey in Time in Celebration of the Millennium.* This book was presented at Ludlow Assembly Rooms during Festival Fortnight and for the succeeding fortnight, attracting enormous interest. We would like to cite two of the comments made in the Visitors Book, partly because they reflect the sentiments of many visitors, both Ludlovians and others, but also because they explain the genesis of this book. *'Absolutely first class! I came twice and, if time had permitted, would have called again. I only wish you had produced a guide with all of the views. A marvellous effort. (Trevor Todd, Great Missenfen, Bucks)*
'A fascinating exhibition, wonderfully presented. This is my third visit so far. A pity it will all be dispersed after the event. Is there any chance of a book of the exhibition being produced?' (Dr Robert Hyde, Knighton, Powys)

We are grateful to Tempus Publishing for acceding to our suggestion that this book, already commissioned, should take on a format that would reflect the exhibition, though we all realise that the black and white reproduction, however good, cannot do justice to some of the colour photographs displayed at the exhibition. We enjoyed mounting the exhibition, though the work involved was prodigious, and we thank the Festival Council for their support, especially Jenny Vaughen. The idea of a millennium exhibition of Ludlow pictures was fundamentally Jenny's and she was the motive force in turning an idea into reality. Part of the dedication in this book to Jenny, shows the respect and affection we both have for her. We also thank everyone at the Assembly Rooms for their help, especially Sally Ford and Walton Brown.

Because this book is essentially a community venture, and because we have both enjoyed its preparation, it is our wish that half of the royalties should go towards the Teme Weirs Trust, a body set up some years ago to conserve two of the town's historic wiers. David Lloyd played a part in establishing the Trust and Gareth has been a committee member throughout, but we are both aware of the dedicated work done by others to steer this project along on the face of many difficulties. We thank particularly the two successive chairman, Tom Caulcott and Alan Poulton, but we believe no one will grudge a special mention for Daphne Jones, who has led the fund-raising in a most imaginative way. The videos she has produced are an enduring memory of this most precious of towns in the twentieth century and we hope this book, covering the same period in a different medium, will stand beside them in the homes of all those who love this town as much as we do. In among her other good works, Daphne has found time to give a great deal of help to us in the preparation of this book, and we have dedicated it in part to her.

David Lloyd and Gareth Thomas
October 2000

One
1900-1909

Illustrations in this chapter show something of Ludlow society at the beginning of the twentieth century, especially the different kinds of housing and living conditions. The Boer War and its aftermath – which included the formation of the Boy Scouts and the Girl Guides – is well recorded, as are a number of leisure pursuits, especially team games. The final picture, of the popular annual regatta, is a further reminder that our Edwardian forbears knew how to enjoy themselves, in spite of the hard lives which many of them led.

This photograph, taken from the bottom of the Lower Wood Road, gives the picturesque view of Edwardian Ludlow, much loved by local residents, visitors and the publishers of postcards. Such images nearly always include the castle which is the largest relic of the town's medieval importance, but they reveal little of the town's social character or economic functions.

Photographed by Jane Green, this view of Lower Broad Street, as seen through the archway of the medieval Broad Gate, shows a picturesque winter scene. In reality, there was great poverty and often poor sanitation in many of the crowded yards behind the street frontages, of what was traditionally a working part of the town.

In 1900 British Imperialism was rampant, encouraged by the military successes of the last two hundred years. The Russian cannon in Castle Gardens – a landmark in the town throughout the twentieth century – was a symbol of this militarism. The cannon had been received as a gift from the Government in 1857, 'on application by the Mayor'. Most Ludlow people were proud of this trophy, though the travel writer Walter White, in his *All Round the Wrekin* (1860), condemned it as 'an eyesore' and 'an ugly thing'.

The Boer War has been regarded by some as one of the least justifiable of Britain's imperial wars and had aroused much contemporary criticism, especially from the politician David Lloyd George. Many local people showed great patriotic fervour, however, and by late December 1899, forty-eight men of the Ludlow Squadron of the Shropshire Yeomanry had already volunteered. This photograph by Robert Sweetman shows one such recruit, proudly wearing his Yeomanry uniform. It was of this kind of soldier that A.E. Housman wrote about in *The Shropshire Lad*, published 1896:

Leave your home behind, lad,
And reach your friends your hand,
And go, and luck go with you,
While Ludlow tower shall stand.

11

A photograph by Jane Green, showing smartly dressed ladies picnicking near Ludlow. In Britain, one of the world's most industrialized nations, eating *al fresco* had become the height of fashion, harking back to what was perceived as an idealized bucolic lifestyle.

Left: A back yard in Corve Street, on part of what is now the site of Tesco (the house was No. 119). This scene typifies the conditions where many of the poorer sections of society lived. *Right:* Jane Green is seen here taking one of her photographs, using a plate camera mounted on a tripod. She is focusing on the glass screen at the rear of the camera, prior to replacing it with a sensitive plate.

At the turn of the twentieth century Ludlow had three football clubs – Ludlow Athletic which is seen here; the Half Holiday Club; and St George's. A meeting had been called in 1899 to merge the clubs in order to create a team strong enough to play in the Herefordshire League. However at the time none of the clubs was prepared to give up their independence, although later on they did join forces, becoming Ludlow Town.

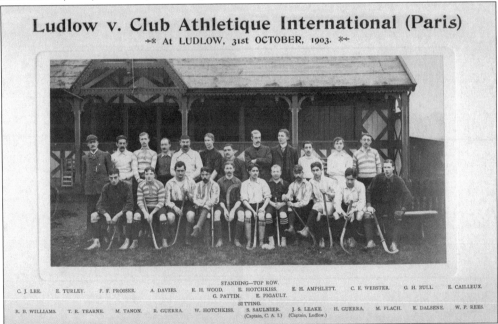

Ludlow v. Club Athletique International (Paris)
→* At LUDLOW, 31st OCTOBER, 1903. *←

STANDING—TOP ROW.
C. J. LEE.   E. TURLEY.   F. F. PROSSER.   A. DAVIES.   E. H. WOOD.   E. HOTCHKISS.   E. H. AMPHLETT.   C. E. WEBSTER.   G. H. BULL.   E. CAILLEUX.
G. PATTIN.   E. PIGAULT.
SITTING.
R. B. WILLIAMS.   T. R. TEARNE.   M. TANON.   R. GUERRA.   W. HOTCHKISS.   S. SAULNIER.   J. S. LEAKE.   H. GUERRA.   M. FLACH.   E. DALSENE.   W. P. REES.
(Captain, C. A. I.)   (Captain, Ludlow.)

A match between Ludlow Hockey Club, formed in 1896, and a visiting team from Paris, photographed in front of the pavilion at Burway. The fixture was probably arranged by Monsieur Guerra, one of the French players, who was temporarily on the staff of Ludlow Grammar School. Is this a faint echo of the entente cordiale between Great Britain and France then being promoted by Edward VII?

13

A plaster cast of the bronze memorial dedicated to the soldiers from South Australia who died in the Boer War, presented to the Borough of Ludlow in 1904 by the sculptor, Capt. Adrian Jones, a native of the town. The Horse stood proudly in the Town Hall, a well-loved though rather over-powering feature. The inset shows the statue itself still in the heart of Adelaide.

Adrian Jones was born in Ludlow in 1845, the son of a veterinary surgeon. He was a pupil at Ludlow Grammar School, who went on to have a military career before becoming a well-known and fashionable sculptor, specialising in equestrian statues. There are many of his works in London, including The Quadriga at Hyde Park Corner. The photograph shows him at work on his model for the Cavalry Memorial in Hyde Park which commemorates all the British Empire's cavalrymen who fell in the First World War. A mounted armoured St George in his twofold character of knight and saint holds aloft his sword, with the slain dragon beneath him, symbolising the defeat of tyranny. Adrian Jones, who died in 1938 at the age of ninety-three, is commemorated by a tablet on the north wall of St Laurence's parish church.

The photographs on this page were taken by or for the Ludlow chemist, Robert Sweetman, and have been printed from the original glass plates. This view shows Sweetman with his bicycle in the churchyard, outside the Reader's House.

Left: Sweetman's chemist shop, established as a family business around 1878, survived for almost all of the twentieth century, latterly in the ownership of R.K. Mellings. *Right*: This view up Broad Street shows Sweetman's shop, on a narrow site seen immediately east of the Butter Cross. In earlier times there was a house here for the parish sexton.

A number of Sunday school classes are gathered together in the Town Hall, although the occasion is unknown. Sunday Schools had been established in Ludlow in the early nineteenth century, and played an important role in bringing a basic education to poor children. By the twentieth century their purpose was largely religious, with winter treats and summer sports an important part of the annual programme.

These are children from the Girls' National School in Lower Galdeford (now the Bishop Mascall Centre). One of the practical subjects taught was gardening which was part of a promotion of 'Cottage Gardening' aiming to make humble households more self-sufficient. Defending this kind of curriculum, one contemporary famously remarked: 'I deplore children being taught the difference between a lion and a whale, in case they should meet either of them on their way home from school. I would rather have them know the difference between turnip seeds and charlock.'

Left: Edward Turford, a leading Ludlow builder, was one of the proprietors of the firm Turford and Southward. They had their yard in Upper Galdeford, a property now occupied by Buftons, agricultural engineers. *Right:* The North and South Wales Bank in the Bull Ring (later the Midland Bank), which was built by Turford and Southward and opened in 1908. The mock Tudor style was popular at this time.

The large house in Gravel Hill which was built by Edward Turford for his own family. Many of the imposing residences in Gravel Hill and neighbouring roads were constructed by Turford and Southward, often for the town's successful businessmen. The house was initially called Newlands, but the name was changed to Alexandra House when it became a nursing home for the elderly.

In the Edwardian period, Ludlow had a number of large families, some of them with descendants who remained in the town throughout the century. One such example is the family of William Lloyd, the lamplighter, who can be seen at the back of this picture. Sitting on the far right is James (Jim) Lloyd, who later became the custodian of Ludlow Castle, and whose son Bob was caretaker at Ludlow School.

Through the centuries many Ludlow people have found marriage partners from the surrounding area. Thomas Cooper, who worked for much of his life as a baker for Davies and Brown of No. 7 Castle Street, is seen with his bride, Agnes Deakin. She was one of the daughters of James Deakin, a farm worker at Pipe Aston, a small parish in Herefordshire, some four miles out of Ludlow on the Wigmore Road.

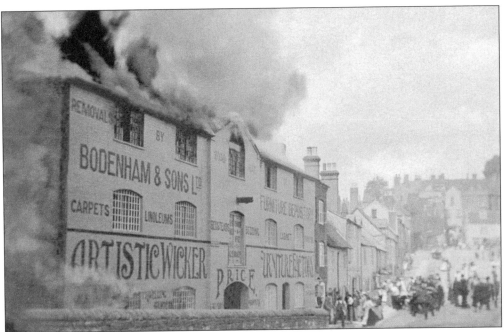

Ludlow has escaped a major fire, such as that which destroyed much of Warwick in 1694. However a small fire in 1908 damaged a building which had been built in the nineteenth century for William Evans, Ludlow's last large scale cloth manufacturer. It then became a warehouse for Bodenham & Sons, Ltd, who were house furnishers, storage and removal contractors, as well as drapers and outfitters.

The furniture in the street may have come from the warehouse, but it is more likely that it belonged to neighbours, who moved it outside in case the fire should spread.

The Ludlow Boy Scouts are seen mounting a display of drill and other skills, in front of a large audience on the Castle Green. The Boy Scouts were founded in 1907 by Robert Baden-Powell, a hero of the siege of Mafeking in the Boer War. His book, *Scouting for Boys*, published in 1908, quickly led to the formation of troops all over the country. According to The Scout Law, boys had to be: trustworthy, loyal, helpful, friendly, courteous, kind, obedient, cheerful, thrifty, brave, clean and reverent.

Another kind of spectacle was provided by the annual regatta, held on the River Teme. Spectators, many of them in their best clothes, line the banks at the Bread Walk, just below Dinham Bridge.

Two
1910-1919

Though Edward VII died in 1910, the early part of the decade was essentially a continuation of the Edwardian years. The first pictures show the normality of Ludlow life – the hay harvest, a coach excursion, the lamplighter at work – though the opening of the town's third garage was a portent of the motor revolution to come later on in the century. In 1914 the shock waves reverberating across Europe embraced the town and it was caught up in the maelstrom of the First World War.

This photograph of mounted soldiers of the South Shropshire Yeomanry outside the New Inn in Upper Galdeford, gives a foretaste of the impact of war. It also gives a rare glimpse of the town's fire station, which for a few years was on council owned land that had formerly been the pound or pinfold – the enclosure where stray animals were impounded. On the far right is William Price, a plumber whose grand-children and great-grand-children still live in the town.

Funeral of His (late) Most Gracious Majesty
KING EDWARD VII.

Memorial Service

IN THE

CHURCH OF SAINT LAWRENCE, LUDLOW,

On Friday, the 20th day of May, 1910,

At 1-30 o'clock in the Afternoon,

instead of 1 o'clock as advertised, in consequence of alteration in arrangements at Windsor.

Order of the Procession.

1 Fire Brigade
2 "G" Company 4th Battalion Kings Shropshire Light Infantry
3 Boy Scouts
4 Church Lads' Brigade
5 Friendly Societies
6 Masters of the National and British Schools
7 Committees of these Schools
8 Grammar School with Masters
9 Board of Guardians and Rural District Council
10 Ludlow Agricultural Society
11 Charity Trustees and Governors of the Ludlow Grammar School
12 The Free-Masons
13 Town Crier
14 Borough Officials
15 Mace Bearer
16 Councillors in order of Seniority
17 Mace Bearer
18 Aldermen
19 Clerk of the Peace
20 Borough and County Magistrates
21 The Mace Bearer
22 Mayor, Deputy Mayor and Town Clerk

NOTE. The Procession will leave the Church in the reverse order, the Mayor leading.

This poster advertised the local memorial service for King Edward VII, held when his body was buried in the vault of St George's chapel, Windsor, after lying in state at Westminster for four days. It gives a revealing glimpse of the hierarchy of Ludlow organizations, culminating with the Mayor, at that time the chemist, George Woodhouse.

Farming was still an important activity on the fringes of Ludlow, as shown by this hay harvest scene in a field adjoining Livesey Road. The field was part of the farm attached to Overmead House, owned by the Ludlow grocer, Gaius Smith. The man on the left on top of the wagon was William Parker, Gaius Smith's bailiff. Several people on the photograph, like Gaius Smith himself, were active members of the Methodist church.

A horse drawn coach, being used for an outing by members of the Licensed Victuallers Association. One of these was Frederick William Curtis, landlord of the Star Hotel (later the Star and Garter) seen on the far right of the photograph.

Corve Garage, described as 'motor, cycle and general engineers', opened at No. 29 Corve Street in 1912, joining Temeside Garage and Ludlow Motor Garage at No. 141 Corve Street, which had started a few years previously. Motor vehicles brought many benefits to Ludlow and also created problems that were still unresolved at the end of the century; but at first cars were envied curiosities.

Woodhouse's chemist shop at No. 45 Bull Ring. Woodhouse had been Mayor when the Princess of Wales, later Queen Mary, came to Ludlow in 1909, and her patronage of his shop – the tradition is that she bought a tooth-brush – entitled him to display the royal arms. The business was later acquired by Boots.

William Lloyd the lamplighter, (already featured on p. 18) is here seen at work, ascending on his ladder to adjust one of the gaslights in Mill Street. Jack Gatehouse, son of Alderman Albert Gatehouse the grocer, writing about his Ludlow childhood a few years later, recalled that the lamplighter did his nightly round pulling the tap levers with his long rod to produce the flickering yellow light in the street. This picture has been enlarged from a postcard lent by Harvey Griffiths, one of the many grandchildren of William Lloyd.

This view of Mary's Meadow, a Victorian house with a large garden on Temeside, comes from the frontispiece of *Mary's Meadow Papers*, written in 1912, and published in 1915. The book, a collection of spiritual essays, was written by Mrs Violet O'Connor (nee Bullock-Webster), who had settled in Ludlow some years previously with her husband Armel and her small daughter Betty. Both the O'Connors published a number of poems and religious books from Mary's Meadow, all of them proclaiming the Roman Catholic Church, of which they were zealous Ludlow members. Their lifestyle and philosophies – they taught Betty at home – elicited some local sympathy and support, though there was also derision and misunderstanding.

Armel O'Connor was a gifted musician, who taught singing at Ludlow Grammar School for many years. One of his colleagues was the French master, George Merchant, to whom he later dedicated one of his books of poems, *Candles in the Night*. One of the poems was entitled, 'The Dreamers':

We'd lose our lives with shouts of joy
If man would only start again,
Be God's own tools; in His employ
Bring low the hill, exalt the plain,

If noble dreams were proven true,
And life shown worth its bitter pain;
We'd risk a broken heart or two
Broken but not in vain.

People of many ages, occupations and social groups were in Castle Square on 4 August 1914, to hear the Mayor announce that war had been declared against Germany. There was anxiety on many faces, but the mood in the town was resolute and at times exuberant. Many people saw the war as a righteous crusade, among them the authoress of a book on the war published in 1915 'for boys and girls'. 'The soldiers of the Allies went out to battle … like knights of old, full of anger against an enemy who was fighting unjustly, and full, too, of a determination to fight their best for justice and right. This is one reason which has made the Great War … so wonderful a thing.'

Thomas and Mary Lowe of The Queen's Arms (now The Bridge) in lower Corve Street in 1915, with their five children, one of whom, William, had enlisted in the King's Shropshire Light Infantry, and later fought at Ypres. In 1915 the country was still gripped with patriotic fervour and families, though apprehensive, were proud of those who volunteered.

The Ludlow Troop of the Shropshire Yeomanry, before they were ordered overseas. The photograph was taken at the race course stables at Bromfield, where their horses were kept. The commanding officer was Maj. J.P.H. Heywood-Lonsdale. Third from the left on the back row is David John, a well-known local farmer.

Three soldiers of the Ludlow Troop of the Shropshire Yeomanry, enjoying a short leave in Egypt in 1916. They were part of a force sent to the Middle East to check German expansion into this area. This was a posed photograph, proudly sent to relatives at home. From left to right: Clement Roberts, a Ludlow bank clerk; Bernard Davies from Wistanstow; David John from Stanton Lacy.

All over the country, women took over jobs formerly done by men who had gone into the armed forces. Many of those who worked on farms joined the Land Girls. This is Mary Corfield, who worked on a farm in Halford, just outside Craven Arms. She later married Dick Howard, who after the war had a fruit and vegetable business on Bromfield Road, then a shop in Church Street.

Overmead, built soon after 1900 for the King Street grocer and former Mayor, Gaius Smith, was one of Ludlow's largest houses. It stood in spacious grounds off Livesey Road, itself named after Smith's wife. During the war it was made available to the Red Cross as a convalescent home for wounded servicemen, several of whom can be seen in front of the house. The croquet hoops and mallets, marks of a leisured and elegant life style, are in ironic contrast to the horrors of the Western Front, where many of these men had been injured.

The war came unusually close to Ludlow in 1918, when a Camel aircraft used for advertising War Bonds, based at Shawbury, crashed on the racecourse at Ludlow, attracting a large crowd of sight-seers.
By a bizarre coincidence a young man from Bromfield, Tom Mellings, flew a Camel aricraft for the RAF on the Western Front where he was killed in action on 20 July 1918. In his short career – he was twenty when he died – he destroyed fifteen enemy aircraft, and won the DAC (with Bar) and the DFC.

Peace was announced in Castle Square on 11 November 1918, by the Mayor, Alderman Edward Sheldon. He was accompanied by other members of the borough council and by the town clerk, J.H. Williams. The civic party is preceded by the mace-bearers, the town crier and the Clerk of the Market. The wives of councillors watch from the balcony of the Council Chamber in the Town Hall where the Union Jack is hanging. The town's first cinema, which opened in the Assembly Rooms in 1909, can be seen on the right.

A celebratory meal for ex-service men in the Town Hall, provided by the British Legion. Patriotic flags were displayed but the mood seems subdued, perhaps out of respect for the 117 Ludlow men who had died in the First World War.

Three
1920-1929

The pictures in this chapter illustrate some aspects of Ludlow's economy, including its hotels and the links with the surrounding countryside. The most revealing is one of the town's many domestic gardens, where much of the local food supply was produced. Horses were still common in the town, but motor transport was increasing. Leisure activities, as well as school and youth groups, have also been recorded. However, storm clouds were already gathering over Europe, and there was a feeling of discontent and injustice in the country. For some, the most evocative photograph will be that of 1926, showing army lorries in Ludlow, probably on their way to an area of industrial unrest, later to escalate into the general strike.

The New Inn, now swathed in ivy – perhaps a sign of wartime neglect. Those gathered here are now young motor-cyclists, an echo of 'the Gay Young Things' who swept through the upper echelons of British society in a mood of post-war freedom and celebration. The caption shows, however, that the New Inn, whose landlord was William Joseph Perry, was also a base for more conventional sports.

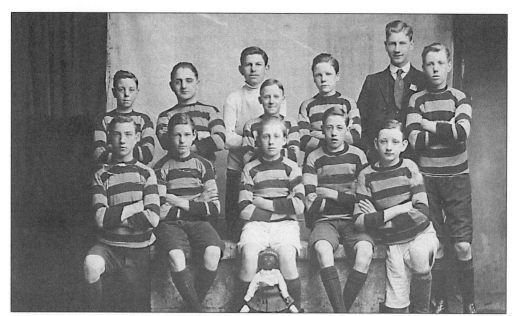

After the First World War, many youth organizations were revitalised, among them 'the Crusaders' who were the young footballers or 'colts' of Ludlow Town. The names of many large and enduring Ludlow families are recognisable. E. Charles (grandfather of Barbara Hall, now of Dartmouth, who owns the photograph), E. Gravenor, T. Devey, V. Parsonage, G. Fisher, T. Fewtrell, L. Davies, ? Price, ? Ward, ? Nunnery, S. Spear, and ? Jones.

'One man and his dog' in a field in Linney. The man has been identified as Edward Good, a veterinary surgeon who lived and practised at No. 21 Corve Street, adjacent to the field. He was described in Kelly's 1922 Trade Directory as 'a canine specialist'. The field, with its cropped grass, was probably pasture, while the hens and the line of low buildings (perhaps pigsties) to the left, suggest that this part of Ludlow was being used for small-time agriculture.

Ludlow Male Voice Choir in 1921, photographed in the outer bailey of Ludlow Castle. The choir gave regular concerts in the Town Hall, with items such as 'Crossing the Bar', 'Early One Morning' and Elgar's *Reveille*. The choir included many of the town's leading citizens, some of them members of the brough council. From left to right, back row: Roy Jones, Gus Lowe, Fred Hill, Harry Lewis, Mr Tomkins, Mr Faulkner, Mr Kenhard, Tom Fewtrell, Mr Elmore, Albert Jones, George Williams, Tommy Wainwright, Mr Wilding. Middle row: Mr Jones, Mr Harper, Arthur Higgins, Harry Cartwright, Mr Weale, Mr Rudd, Jack Sanderson, Philip Sanders, Charlie Garrod, Mr Stephens, Genville Corbishly, Jack Watkins, Mr Smith. Front row: Frank Fisher, Billy Pugh, Gus A.T. Fisher (accompanist), Armel O'Connor (conductor), Cllr Heber Rickards, Alderman Edward Sheldon, Arthur Higgins Snr, Walter Sanders, Len Detheridge.

For many centuries horse-drawn carriers' and farmers' carts had been coming in and out of Ludlow, bringing produce to market and taking a wide range of products back to the countryside. In the mid-1920s these were still a familiar sight, in spite of the increasing importance of motor lorries. The photograph shows Thomas Davies, a farm labourer who worked for Mr Downes of The Butts at Bromfield. He and two other men are standing in Old Street, outside the Green Dragon public house, while the horses, harnessed to a wagon, (out of camera shot), are resting halfway up the hill.

F.W. BEESTON, Lion Mineral Water Works, Ludlow.
Manufacturers of every kind of Mineral Waters, Bottler of Burton Ales & Dublin Stout.
Orders promptly delivered.

Other horse drawn vehicles can be seen in this rare photograph of the Lion Mineral Water Works, operated by F.W. Beeston, behind the Three Horses Inn in Upper Galdeford (part of the site now occupied by Somerfield).

By the mid-1920s several Ludlow businesses were adopting motor transport. The vans and drivers of Gaius Smith and Co. Ltd, the King Street grocers, are lined up in Castle Square for a photograph to be included in the firm's seventy-two page journal, issued quarterly to advertise their goods and services. From small beginnings in the Bull Ring in 1875, Gaius Smith's had become the largest grocery business in the Ludlow district, with nine branches in neighbouring small towns and villages.

Dorothy Edwards, later Mrs Evans, sitting on a friend's motorcycle in Holdgate Fee, at the bottom of Old Street, *c.* 1925. She is outside No. 124, next door to her parents, James and Martha Edwards, who lived at No. 122. 'Jim', like many Ludlow people, had previously worked on the railway, but after an accident he took a part-time job building jump fences at Ludlow Race Course.

Part of the land behind No. 124 Holdgate Fee, showing James and Martha Edwards busy in their garden, watched by Florence, another daughter, and two grandchildren. The produce from domestic gardens, such as the potatoes being gathered here, was an important part of many household economies. The houses of St Johns Road, culminating in the Broad Gate, can be seen behind.

Part of the Bull Ring in 1925, and particularly the Feathers Hotel, which was then, and still is today, the town's most famous timber-framed building. In 1925 it was owned by a former farmer, William Tanner from Aintree, Onibury, and was a popular rendezvous for the more prosperous farmers of the district, especially after Monday market. People from the countryside also provided the custom for Ludlow's shops, most of which were still family businesses at this time.

LUDLOW'S
PREMIER
ATTRACTION!
::
WINTER
GARDEN
CAFE.
::
LUNCHEONS.
TEAS.
ORCHESTRA.
DANCING.
::
PARTIES
CATERED FOR.
::
OPEN SUNDAYS.
::
J. W. PRICE,
PROPRIETOR.

Ingeniously fitted into a limited space at No. 13 Bull Ring, (on the left in the upper picture) the Winter Gardens brought a touch of the exotic to south Shropshire. They were operated by Joseph William Price, in association with his hair-dressing business next door. The decor and the entertainments on offer were an echo of the Palm Court Orchestra type facilities available at spas and seaside resorts.

A fine view of the yard of the Angel Hotel, on the east side of Broad Street. The Angel had been one of the town's leading inns since the early sixteenth century, and was a terminus for passenger and mail coaches in the eighteenth and nineteenth centuries. The surface of the yard was still cobbled, but at the far end a garage had replaced earlier coach houses and stables. The Angel survived as a hotel into the 1990s but is now being converted for mixed usage, including luxury flats.

The front of the Angel, with two elegant eighteenth-century bay windows protruding from the timber framed facade. To the left can be seen the hotel motor car, which met all trains. The proprietor at this time was R. Kenrick Sharp. By 1929 the hotel had the telephone number four.

This unusual photograph shows army trucks in Broad Street in 1926, parked just below the Angel, while soldiers fraternised with local children. They were travelling through Ludlow, perhaps to South Wales, where industrial unrest was great. The strike began in May with the miners, whose slogan was: 'Not a penny off the pay, not a minute on the day.' The strike later spread to thousands of other workers, necessitating emergency measures to sustain public services.

Uniformed organizations thrived, being seen as a way to inculcate the kinds of behaviour which the promoters deemed desirable. One of the most active in Ludlow was The Church Lads Brigade. Members are lined up for a bicycle ride under the direction of their captain, the Revd R.E. Rogerson, curate. One of his predecessors wrote in Ludlow Parish Magazine: 'We only want smart active boys. The more clumsy and awkward ones may be accepted later when we are more forward with our drill and organization. The smart boys will then help the others to become smart.'

A different kind of regimentation can be seen here, with the girls of one of the upper classes at East Hamlet Church of England Primary School. From left to right, back row: Kathleen Higgins, Connie Collier, Olive Whittle, Dorothy Pugh, Edna Fitzjohn, Phyllis Williams, Phyllis Hawthorne. Middle row: Gertie Perks, Daisie Peachey, Dorothy Gennoe, Lilly Angell, Lucy Hughes, Sarah Cooke. Front row: Kathleen Fitzjohn, Ena Burton, Gladys Steenton, Hilda Garrod, Daisy Davidson, Mary Davies, Joan Harper. The photograph was donated by Ena Burton, the daughter of Harold Burton, headmaster of Ludlow Senior School.

Governors, masters, parents and boys gathered for the laying of three large foundation blocks for an impressive range of new buildings at Ludlow Grammar School in 1928. There were about 130 boys at the school, for most of whom parents paid fees, though a few held scholarships.

The Revd A.E. Lloyd Kenyon, Rector of Ludlow and chairman of the governors for the previous ten years, dedicating one of the foundation blocks. The headmaster, A.C. Telfer, a Cambridge athletics blue can be seen to the right. The French master, George Merchant, later wrote of this period: 'In retrospect the rather lazy years between the wars, free from alarums and excursions, seem indeed to have been like the Golden Age. Unemployment lay like a blight on the land and the international clouds were beginning to gather, black and menacing, but at the bottom of Mill Street we had total employment and had never had it so good.'

In the first part of the twentieth century Ludlow had a few big shops, such as J. Evans and Sons, drapers, which occupied Nos 1, 2, 4 and 5 King Street. However most retailers had smaller premises and employed fewer staff. The two shops shown here were typical of the medium sized establishments in the town centre. One was the shop of James G. Lang, general draper, at No. 1 Castle Street; the premises were later occupied by Woolworths. Unusually, the proprietor was a Doctor of Science, who served as Honorary Curator of Ludlow Museum, where he spent much of his time – allegedly to the neglect of the business.

The Star Supply Stores, grocers, at No. 67 Broad Street, now occupied by James and Co., outfitters. This was one of the first chain stores to be established in Ludlow. On the far left is Ern Evans, who later worked at Peacheys and was the father of Daphne Jones, who has supplied this and several other photographs in this book. On the right of the entrance is the manager, Mr Pugh.

Four

1930-1939

The later pages in this chapter show that quite modest houses did have large gardens, conditions were generally much better in the town's early council houses, and some professional families enjoyed a very high standard of life. There are other pictures to show that living in Ludlow could be most pleasurable, though in the background the threats of international conflict continued to loom.

This picture showing a small boy in Raven Lane in 1938, catches something of the dinginess and claustrophobia of Ludlow's narrowest streets, leading off from which there were many crowded and often insanitary yards. A curate at the parish church offended many people when he spoke from the pulpit, of poor housing conditions in the town.

How can residents sit and listen to the church bells playing Home Sweet Home, while they knew that a hundred yeards away people lived in hovels where pools of water poured in through the roofs.

The two pictures on this page were published for Davies and Brown, millers and bakers, who had a shop at No. 7 Castle Street (now Prices). The Castle mills, though not as old as those further down the River Teme, had been used for grinding corn since the fourteenth century. The mill itself with its wheel, is to the left of this picture, while there is a complex of warehouses and cottages to the right. The area was later the site of the town's first swimming pool (see p. 81) but this has recently been demolished and replaced by a millennium green, after massive local effort and fund-raising.

The ancilliary buildings of the mill complex, seen from the junction of Dinham and Linney.

Two views of the River Teme and its weirs, once the major source of industrial power for medieval and early modern Ludlow and now a delight for residents and visitors alike. *Top left:* Steventon Weir can be seen which was used to service the Case Mill in 1930 (visible to the left of the trees). The mill was so called because it produced small boxes or cases for jewellery. The young women were Betty Stephens and Eileen Stephens (not related). *Top right:* shows part of the Bread Walk, with the Minett family taking a stroll. Beyond is Dinham Bridge, upstream of which is Dinham Weir.

LW. 120 RIVER AND CLEE HILL, LUDLOW

Mill Street weir, beyond which can be seen the pumping engine and water works. A lone fishermen plies his rod in the turbulent water below the weir.

This image has been reproduced from a painting of the north side of High Street, focusing on the shop of George Pearce, fishmonger, game dealer and fruiterer. The artist was Leslie Ward, a teacher from Bournemouth, who often exhibited at the Royal Academy. Ludlow was, and still is, a favourite venue for artists, and pictures of the town feature in many galleries and collections.

A branch of Woolworths opened in 1930, occupying the former premises of Lang's at No. 1 Castle Street (see p. 44). This picture uses the Woolworths' sign, taken from one photograph, with a picture of staff on a day out, taken from another photograph. The outing occurred in 1933.

A group bonded by leisure, not work, at the pavilion of the Ludlow Castle Bowling and Tennis Club in Linney, 1935.

49

This picture was taken in 1934 by Richmond Williams, a Customs and Excise Officer from Swansea, who was a talented amateur photographer. He was also the maternal grandfather of Gareth Thomas. He is seen here on Whitcliffe with his car, a 1931 style twelve horsepower Rover, and his fellow travellers, also members of the Williams family. The view of Ludlow shows residential expansion east of the historic town, including the new council estate at Sandpits Avenue.

An event held on this part of Whitcliffe a few years earlier was a revivalist religious rally. The lorry, a Ford Model T, was owned by George Foster of Leominster, a preacher at the Gospel Hall.

50

The Pageant, presented to raise funds for Shropshire's hospitals, was organized on a county basis, but was staged in Ludlow Castle to mark the tercentenary of the first production there of Milton's *Comus*. As well as a repeat performance of the masque, there were five episodes of Shropshire's history, involving a huge cast, mostly of local amateurs. The event was an important step in the development of Ludlow as a major centre for the performing arts.

SOLE OFFICIAL SOUVENIR & PROGRAMME

1/-

SHROPSHIRE HISTORICAL PAGEANT
& COMUS TERCENTENARY PERFORMANCES
AT LUDLOW CASTLE JULY 2ND-7TH 1934

Two Ludlow people who participated as Silures in the betrayal of Caractacus to the Romans, were Mrs Gladys Potter, later a well known councillor, and her daughter Celia, now Mrs Celia Rowlands, JP. Stories and anecdotes about the pageant circulated in Ludlow for many years, ranging from the plausible to the implausible, e. g. that all the working horses in the town stood still when the Silures and Brigantes shouted 'Woe, Woe'.

Top left: Elizabeth Davies, a war widow, who lived at No. 47 in 1935. *Top right*: Elizabeth's daughter, Doris, in the garden of the same house, looking towards the small shop in Sandpits Road.
Bottom left: Doris a few years later, at the gate of No. 47. *Bottom right*: Bryan Bufton, a baker at De Greys, who lived nearly opposite, first at No. 54, then at No. 48. Bryan Bufton and Doris Davies later married and had one son, Vincent, now a well-known local journalist.

The 1920s and 1930s saw a great expansion of municipal housing, stimulated by the post-war 'Homes Fit for Heroes' campaign. One of Ludlow's council estates was at Sandpits Avenue, which took on the boomerang shape of a field owned by Ludlow Borough Corporation since the fifteenth century. The well-kept gardens and neatly cut hedges indicate caring tenants but in later years the estate had a number of problems, before a regeneration programme in the 1990s. The estate has always had a strong sense of community and nowhere in Ludlow had better street parties in 1945, 1953 and 1977.

The grass in the outer bailey of the castle is being cut by George Morris Jnr (on the vehicle) and his father George Morris Snr (holding the scythe). The Morris family kept the Greyhound Inn in Upper Galdeford, and also operated a haulage business, which started when they transported coal from Clee Hill.

The Coronation on 12 May 1937 of King George VI and Queen Elizabeth gave a rare opportunity for national jollification amidst the anxieties of the mid-1930s. One of the entries for a carnival at Ludlow was this portrayal of a nanny and baby, lavishly decorated with Union Jacks and other patriotic insignia. The nanny was Yvonne Nixon, daughter of the manager of the International Stores. The baby was Clive Jones, son of A.E. Jones, baker, of No. 9 Bell Lane.

William Lloyd, (previously seen on pp 18 and 25), patrolling as a car park attendant in front of Quality Square, though without the ominous note book and biro carried by Traffic Wardens in later years. Behind can be seen the premises of J.C. Austen & Son, printers, and the congested ironmonger's shop of William Price, plumber, and his family. The year was probably 1938.

Some people contrived to live in a luxurious style in pre-war Ludlow. Among them were Dr Thomas Hunter, formerly of the Indian Medical Service, and his wife Jesse. During their Ludlow years, from 1928-1945, they lived at Brand House, where they 'dressed every evening for dinner', and were attended by a cook, housemaid, parlour maid, chauffeur and a gardener. The photograph shows the rear of the house, with part of the spacious garden.

Another glimpse at High Society was at Castle House in 1938, where employees of the Earl of Powis, the owner, are providing a Christmas party for children. The servants' uniforms, the cabinet bookcases, the plaster frieze and the large windows with their heavy curtains hint at a lifestyle enjoyed earlier in the century, when this was the residence of Robert Marston, Esq., solicitor.

Ludlow's first Rugby Football XV, 1935. This developed from a team fielded by the Old Boys of Ludlow Grammar School, when the game was introduced in 1928. The club thrived after the Second World War, eventually having four teams. From left to right, back row: C. Jurd (a visiting Frenchman, who later became part of the French resistance), ? Boycott, B. Wightman, G. Merchant, ? Gwynn, ? Lovekin, H. Davies, H.T. Baker, ? Stansfield, G. Robinson (secretary). Middle row: G. Davies, ? Marsh, ? Bruford (captain), J. Sturton, B. Williams. Front row: M. Connolly, A. David (games master at the Grammar school).

Singing in the St Laurence's parish church choir, where the tradition of choral music, was still strong, went back to the Middle Ages. The organist and choirmaster 1917-1948 was the redoubtable Frank Bastick, who himself had been a chorister at St Paul's Cathedral. This photograph was taken in 1939. From left to right, back row: P. Baker (churchwarden), I. Wilkes, D.N. La Touche, A.G. Jones, T.T. Price, C.E. Judd, R.E. Jones, W. Shaw, H. Burton (headmaster of the National Senior School), T.J. Evans, T. Owen, H.J. Price, R.G. Brookes (verger), T.F. Saunders (churchwarden). Middle row: L. Morris, I. Reynolds, J. Batty, F.E. Bastick (organist and choirmaster), Revd G.W. Whitlock (preacher), Prebendary F.G. Shepherd (rector), Revd W. Wallace, E.W. Lethbridge, C. Everall, J. Langley, G. Baker, W. Matthews. Front row: K. Lucas, D. Reynolds, P. Morris, M. Heath, B. Edwards, C. Price, F. Hiles, A. Heath, A. Matthews, B. Weaver, S. Cowell, A. Elliott, H. Devey.

Five
1940-1949

This decade saw years of war and post-war austerity. Although Ludlow saw little direct action – only one unexploded bomb – the war affected the whole community with rationing, shortages and blackouts, as it did throughout the country. Airmen and soldiers, including personable American GIs, were stationed at Ludford Park and elsewhere in the vicinity. Young men and women, drafted into the forces or other forms of war work, often travelled great distances, many of them travelling abroad for the first time. Attitudes changed and some class divisions were broken down. There was heartache and tragic loss, and the memorial boards in St Laurence's record the deaths of thirty-eight Ludlow men. Yet in the face of adversity there was great camaraderie, and many elderly people in Ludlow today remember the war fondly, in spite of the dangers and sorrows.

This picture, taken in 1946, catches something of the war spirit. In the centre is Cyril Morgan and to his right, his brother-in-law Robert Glaze. Both had fought their way through Italy with the North Staffordshire Infantry, seconded to the American Fifth Army. They had fought at Anzio and been in Rome when Gen. Mark Clark made his triumphal entry on 6 June coinciding with D-Day. On their left is William Glaze, Robert's younger brother, who was doing his National Service with the Royal Navy, later to see service in the Mediterranean on *HMS Arthur*. Such family groups would have been seen in all parts of Ludlow.

Evacuees from Liverpool, the West Midlands and elsewhere flooded into Ludlow and the surrounding countryside in 1939 and 1940. Some were unhappy, but many discovered a rewarding new life and remained in Ludlow after the war. The children shown here, Jennifer Mundy (left) and her cousins Jill and Carl Westmeads enjoyed their evacuee experience. They are romping happily near their new home in the peaceful village of Bouldon, a few miles outside Ludlow, oblivious of the slaughter and horror in other parts of the world.

The same children as in the previous photograph, sitting on a farm wagon. After the war Albert Westmeads and his brother Harry opened the Meads Engineering factory off Bromfield Road, with Len Mundy as works manager. The company, one of the first to provide industrial employment in Ludlow in the immediate post-war period, manufactured paraffin pressure lamps, stoves and blow lamps.

HMS *Ludlow*, one of fifty First World War destroyers given to Great Britain by the United States in return for naval bases in the Caribbean. This was a way for providing American support without, at that stage, direct participation in the war. She was renamed in accordance with the Admiralty's decision to call the ships after towns in both Britain and the USA. The ship's silk White Ensign, made by the ladies of Ludlow, now hangs in the parish church.

A 1941 poster, only part of which is shown here, typifies efforts made at home in support of the war effort. The collection of salvage was only one of many contributions. Another campaign was 'Dig for Victory', with intense cultivation of gardens and allotments. Money saving was encouraged, as in 'Wings for Victory' weeks. Queues became a feature of local life, as Ludlow housewives learnt to deal with food shortages and rationing.

YOUR PART

in the Battle of the Atlantic

THE Battle of the Atlantic is a battle for supplies—supplies which mean victory if we get them, and defeat if we don't. The collection of salvage plays a direct part in that vital struggle. Every ton of waste which we salvage is a victory in itself: it saves shipping space; it may save English lives.

A year ago Ludlow held its first special salvage week. The response was magnificent. Almost every house provided its quota. The Town Council is making another appeal. The need is now even greater. There must still be hundreds of tons of salvage of various kinds in our attics and cellars, in corners and cupboards. We need them all.

Will you look for your share and get it ready for the Corporation lorry? **Without** your help we can do nothing: but **with** your help we can turn rubbish into the tools for victory.

Ludlow's Special Salvage Week
Starting on Monday, June 30th

These are the things we ask you to have ready :

SCRAP METAL
of all kinds,

RAGS
these are specially needed,

USED DRY BATTERIES
both large and small,

JAM JARS
We want over 10,000 of them

and

BOTTLES
any kind, except broken ones.

Turn them out and get them ready before you forget about it

A Corporation lorry will call at every house in the town. As far as may be possible, the following streets will be visited on the days given :

Monday, June 30th
Upper Galdeford, Gravel Hill, Livesey Road, Sandpits Avenue, Rock Lane, Sandpits Road, Julian Road, Henley Road, Rocks Green, Dodmore Lane, New Street, Castle View, Belle Vue, New Road, Fishmore.

Wednesday, July 2nd
Raven Lane, Bell Lane, Silk Mill Lane, Mill Street, High Street, King Street, Market Street, Church Street, Camp Lane.

Tuesday, July 1st
Lower Galdeford, Sheet Road, Steventon New Road, Temeside, Old Street, Brand Lane, St. John's Lane and Road, Broad Street, Lower Broad Street.

Thursday, July 3rd
Dinham, Linney, Corve Street, Bromfield Road, St. Mary's Lane, Station Drive, Portcullis Lane, Tower Street, College Street, and any other places not specially mentioned above.

PAPER

The demand for waste paper is becoming more and more urgent. A Corporation lorry tours the town collecting paper on every second and fourth Friday of the month. We beg of you that you will save every scrap of paper and turn out every unwanted magazine or book for these collections. If the lorry does not call at your house regularly, then stop it, or send a note to the Borough Surveyor at the Guildhall.

"Ludlow Advertiser"

The tranquillity of Dinham Bridge, photographed 'during the war' by Alan Hopkins of Leintwardine, was rudely shattered on 16 May 1943, when No. 1 Platoon (Ludlow) Company of the Shropshire Home Guard, staged a mock 'Battle of Dinham', watched by cheering crowds on the castle walks. Before the proceedings there was a radio broadcast, magnified by loud speaker, given by the platoon commander, Capt. A.W. Churchill. This was worthy, it was said, of his namesake, the Prime Minister, currently visiting President Roosevelt in the United States: 'Hello Great Britain, Hello the British Empire, Hello America, Is that you Washington? If so, please thank our Prime Minister for his greeting to us from the White House in which he urged us to keep burning the light of freedom and guard it well. In this West Midland town of Shropshire, set in a gem of English scenery, that, Sir, is what we are doing. If the Nazis drop upon us from the skies, they will truly find that they have come down in the lion's den. As the Prime Minister pointed out, our motto may well be 'Ubique' for we of the Home Guard are everywhere.'

The history of the Ludlow Home Guard was told, after the war, by Capt. Churchill in *From Stand-To to Stand-Down*, who introduced his work with this poem:

> *We fought no fight, we only drilled and waited,*
> *For those invading Nazis who never came,*
> *Our thirst for glory still remains unsated,*
> *No deeds of ours extend the scroll of fame.*
> *But still we gave what time our toil could spare,*
> *And had the summons sounded,*
> *WE WERE THERE.*

On the left is Sydney Hiles, landlord of the Globe Inn, smartly standing guard as a member of the ARP at a hut off Henley Road. On the right a more relaxed attitude is shown by an American GI, Alfie Sweeney, one of several hundred soldiers camping at Ludford Park in preparation for D-Day. Sweeney returned to Ludlow in 1996, when he recalled, 'In the evenings we came into Ludlow, where I enjoyed a few beers in its lovely pubs and we met a lot of locals.' Many Ludlow people still vividly remember the American soldiers, including their baseball matches on the Castle Green and their jitterbugging in Town Hall dances.

Many women took jobs in factories during the war. This is a group at Strongs of Tenbury, who made strikers for bombs. Included are several women from Ludlow: third from left is the wife of Bill Sherry, a Ludlow labourer; fourth from right is Rose Marsh of Holdgate Fee; second from right is Bessy Glaze, and on the far right is Miss Howard, from Holdgate Fee. They travelled to and from Tenbury each day by railway.

B Company of the fourth Battalion of the King's Shropshire Light Infantry on the march in Holland in September 1944, three months after D-Day. Private Harry Smith of Ludlow was at the rear of the left-hand column. Harry was wounded a few months later but survived the war and now lives in Teme Avenue.

Soldiers of the 617 Assault Squadron of the Royal Engineers are seen here in a two day operation in late March 1945, ferrying Sherman tanks across the Rhine. The transporter was being winched back to the western bank to fetch more vehicles. The unit was commanded by Capt. Ellis Shaw, M.C. (seen on the right of the inset), a native of Cheshire who moved to Ludlow after the war to become surveyor to Ludlow RDC and later Chief Technical Services Officer to South Shropshire District Council.

The First Rugby XV, 1945/46, which was one of the best sides Ludlow Grammar School produced, winning fourteen and drawing one of seventeen matches on a strong fixture list. Games had been encouraged at the boys schools since the nineteenth century, in the belief that they promoted team spirit, physical fitness and the values sometimes known as 'muscular Christianity'. Players were: R.J. Skelton (wing), A.R. Gatehouse, (forward), J. Roberts (wing), F.R. Maddocks (forward), H.J. Montlake (forward), C.D. Shelton (centre), J. Steele (forward), A.T. Wakeman (wing forward), R.J. Edwards (forward), R. Dahn (vice-captain and centre), S.R. Montlake (captain and forward), E.G. Onlsow (forward), C.G. Holt (wing), W.J. Bishop (full-back), S.M. Willians (forward), D.R. Potts (scrum half), E.A. Griffiths (fly-half), P.S. Gazey (forward).

Physical games, especially tennis, hockey and netball, were taught at the Girls High School, but in the late 1940s many girls belonged to the Sea Rangers, led by an energetic young geography teacher, Peggy Markes. Here the Rangers pose for a photograph beside the River Teme at Dinham Bridge, while a crew of four raise oars in their boat with Miss Markes at the helm.

The winter of 1946-1947 brought prolonged snowfalls, followed by heavy spring floods. The upper picture shows the Bull Ring being cleared of snow, using a horse pulled cart.

The lower picture shows the River Teme in flood at the lower end of Weeping Cross Lane, with two local residents, Flo Tipton and Lil Nicholas, getting about by rowing boat.

The war and the increased opportunities for higher education brought young people a wider choice of marriage partners. Muriel Bodenham, daughter of a Ludlow outfitter, who had gone from the Girls' High School to take a sociology degree at London University, is seen here at her wedding in 1948 to Peter Curry, a mechanical engineer. They made their home in South Wales but after Peter's premature death, Muriel returned to Ludlow to take over the family business and played a prominent part in the life of the town.

This is a much earlier event, but it affords several points of comparison with the Bodenham marriage seen in the previous photograph. It shows the wedding of Stanley Cowell, a coal carrier, with Edith Wait, daughter of James Wait, coachman at the Feathers. The wedding took place at the parish church on Boxing Day, 1927, followed by a reception for family and close friends at No. 24 Raven Lane, where the brides relatives, Bill and Annie Hardwick, kept a small boarding house.

Members of the Ludlow branch of the Red Cross, seen here with a new ambulance, parked in Castle Square. The picture shows two people who gave Ludlow outstanding service during the middle years of the twentieth century. One from the left is Dr James Egan, a GP who lived at No. 37 Broad Street and received the rare acolade of Freedom of the Borough in 1967. Five from the right is Mrs Florence Robinson, JP, who received the British Empire medal for her work for the Red Cross.

A group of officials and attendants, taken outside the borough council offices at Dinham Lodge at the last Ludlow Quarter Sessions in 1949. The group includes the last Recorder of Ludlow, Judge Meredith, and the town clerk, JP Mallony. The mace bearers were Gwynn Howells (right) and John Evans.

Six
1950-1959

Ludlow in these years was a vibrant, cohesive community, with many clubs and activities for all age groups. It had close links with the surrounding countryside, as shown by the large area occupied by the livestock market (see p. 72) and by the pictures of Cades and Marstons. The transporter (see p. 71) struggling to negotiate Ludford Bridge was a precursor of problems to come, but as the picture shows, a man could still walk his dogs peacefully in a main street. Major defects in the woodwork and masonry of the parish church necessitated a significant restoration campaign from 1952-1959. The dramatic productions mounted to raise some of the required funds brought the town many benefits, and led to the formation of Ludlow Festival in 1960.

The photograph shows the Bull Ring on a typical working day in the 1950s. There are some parked vehicles and a number of shoppers and other pedestrians, but the pace of life seems to be steady, not frenzied. The tall timber-framed buildings reflect the town's historical prosperity. The building on the right is occupied by the national chain store Boots, rather than a local business.

Jack Maddox of Stanton Lacy, a porter at Ludlow railway station, is shown with pigeons which had been sent to Ludlow for release as part of their training programme. 'The Fancy' was a popular sport in Ludlow itself and many Ludlow trainers also used the railway for training and racing their own pigeons. The inset shows the front of the station, the demolition of which by British Rail in the late 1960s was much resented.

The 1st Ludlow Girl Guides are setting off to camp at Saundersfoot, from Ludlow Station in 1950. From left to right, back row: Margaret Bengree, Jean Higgins, Pauline Archer, Vivien Reaves, Dilys Burgoyne, Peggy Burgoyne, Sheila Martin, Betty Pound, Joyce Morris, Kay Marshall, Janet Harper, Pat Threlfall. Front row: Daphne Evans, Lillian Parker, Jackie Harcourt, Barbara Nash, Barbara James, Pat Killworth, Shelia Maddox, Elizabeth Threlfall.

The procession out of the parish church in 1951 is headed by Valerie Morris, Festival Rose Queen in 1951. This was one of a number of annual Rose Queen events organized by Mrs Ernest Lloyd of Gravel Hill, under the auspices of the Methodist church. The year 1951 was an euphoric one for the whole country, with the Festival of Britain planned to give everyone a post-war boost after the years of war and post-war austerity. Valerie was a High School girl who lived in Station Drive. The boy carrying the flag behind her was Gerald Acton, who later became a well-known rugby player and a successful businessman in the colour printing trade.

For some young people in Ludlow, in the 1950s a popular rendezvous was 'under the pines' on Whitcliffe. The picture gives a panoramic view of Gravel Hill, where the most prominent feature is still St Peter's Roman Catholic church, built in the 1930s. Philip Gough was a grammar school boy who later read science at Oxford and had a business career in East Anglia. Vivien Reeves was a High School girl who became an audiologist.

A postcard of the east side of the church yard, showing the historic Reader's House, with its fine timber-framed porch of 1616 and two houses to the left which were built later. In the 1950s the house on the right was Teff's Café, a small heavily furnished room, full of brass ware and Victorian bric-a-brac, tended by the formidable Mrs Harding and her daughter Jean. Young people, including students on vacation, would spend hours here for the price of one cup of tea, putting the world to rights and planning glorious futures – most of which never materialised.

Increasing traffic in the post-war years made the A49 through the centre of Ludlow a very busy road, with the medieval Ludford Bridge a notorious bottleneck. Here a huge transporter lorry was having great difficulty negotiating the awkward corner into Temeside.

In contrast, other parts of the town were very peaceful, including the banks of the River Teme just above Dinham Bridge, a favourite resort for mothers and children on warm summer afternoons. Most of this site was later occupied by the new swimming pool (see p. 81) but the ground has now been restored as a millennium green after prodigious local effort.

This aerial view shows the extent of the northern part of the town in the mid-1950s. The livestock market with its rows of pens, is a prominent feature on the right, while beyond is the railway with its sidings and the branch line to the stone quarries on Clee Hill. On the left can be seen a few houses that were already built in Linney – soon to become a high quality residential area. At the top of the picture is the industrial and commercial estate on Bromfield Road, first developed in the First World War.

One of the businesses on the Bromfield Road Estate was that of Cades, fruit and vegetable merchants. The driver by the middle lorry is Walter Postons, Snr.

A branch of St John's Ambulance Brigade was established in Ludlow before 1934. The picture shows members of the women's section, after an inspection at the Town Hall in 1955. From left to right, back row: Edith Cartwright, Dorothy Wakeman (now Jennings), Barbara Charlton, -?-, Margaret Edwards, ? Whitefoot, Shirley Lloyd, Doreen Cook (now Watkins), -?-, -?-. Front row: May Jackson, Annie Wakeman, Gladys Doeing (superintendent), Gerturde Lewis (now Hall), ? Smith, -?-, ? Smith.

This photograph, taken behind the Queen's Head in Lower Galdeford, shows the Brigade at full strength. Several ladies can be seen in both pictures.

The Whitcliffe Bowling Club, with the captain, plumber Bill Price, sitting proudly in the centre of the group. This was the oldest of the town's three bowling greens, in use since the eighteenth century. Many of the members were on, or employed by, the Borough Corporation, while others were prominent local businessmen. From left to right, back row: Dennis Watkins (Ludlow Motor Co.), -?-, William Bowdler (plumber), Roy Leach, George Stead (grocer), -?-, Ron Thatcher (borough rent collector), Charles Jones (butcher), -?-, -?- (both from Craven Arms), Cyril Hince (gardener at Oakly Park Estate). Middle row: Harry Duce (British Railways), Charles Leach (publican of the Bowling Green Hotel), Harry Cole (publican of the Exchange Vaults), -?-, Stanley Davies (coal merchant), Hugh Badlan (British Railways booking clerk), George Pinches (water board), Fred Harcourt (MEB), Charles Bradley (British Railways), William Mumford (Ludlow Motor Co.), Frank Sherry (borough council works foreman), Charles Haynes (British Railways), 'Jimmy' James (borough surveyor). Front row: Charles Judd (music and radio business proprietor, councillor), Harry Little (Inland Revenue, mayor 1949-52), William Price Snr (retired plumber), Sidney Price (baker, mayor 1954-57, 1961), William Price (captain, plumber, mayor 1965-68), Van Dyke (Veritas, manufactures of lamps and stoves), Joseph Lloyd (policeman), Val Cheadler (banker), ? Croxton (farmer).

Roy Nash, watched by Alec Peachey, concentrates on the serious business of bowling an end, i.e. propelling one of his two bowls towards a jack at the other end of the green.

This lorry, one of the expanding fleet belonging to Norman Lloyd of Ludlow, haulage contractor, has been loaded with sacks of grain from the warehouse of Marston Brothers Ltd, corn, agricultural seed and wool merchants. Marstons was the main firm in south Shropshire for supplying animal feed, fertilizers and other items to local farmers, and for processing grain, wool and other products. Wheat and other cereals were ground on the premises, using an electric hammer mill or a rolling mill, but much of the cavernous building was used for warehousing. The men with the lorry are, from left to right: Harry Rogers, Tom Clee (from Onibury), Matthew Dixon (Whitbread Road), Aubrey Jones (New Street, driver), his son Neville (on the cab).

Families have been the basic units of British society throughout the twentieth century, though there have been changes in relationships within families and between families and society. The nuclear family – husband, wife, children, – was at the core of family networks, but ties to other members of the extended family – grandparents, uncles, aunts and cousins – were also strong. One example of this close family unit in Ludlow is the Tolley family, beginning with Jack, a farm worker, and his wife Emma, who had ten children. Here are three of those children, with Emma, a widow, and some of their own nuclear families: From left to right, back row: Emma Tolley; her daughter-in-law Sheila; her daughter Nancy; Charles Whittal, son-in-law and his wife Beatrice, another of Emma's daughters. Front row: Graham Tolley, son of Christopher and Sheila; Alan Dixon, son of Matthew and Nancy; Charles Tolley, younger son of Christopher and Sheila; and Hilary Dixon, daughter of Matthew and Nancy. Hilary later married Vince Bufton, a well known local journalist, and is now a very active member of the Ludlow community.

The Portlock family, descended from Mr and Mrs Colley Portlock, Bull Ring grocers. Their son Gerald was a passionate horse breeder and entertainer, who performed at circuses and shows. Members of the family are seen here after a fund-raising effort for the Orthopaedic Hospital near Oswestry. From left to right: Betty, daughter of Gerald and her husband Frank Faulkner; Fanny, Gerald's wife; one of the grandsons of Gerald and Fanny; Gerald Portlock; Gertrude, another daughter of Gerald, and her husband Tom Davies, son of Leonard Davies, the Ludlow auctioneer.

Throughout the century, most Ludlow mayors, in his or her first period of office, have been widely recognised as the town's first citizen, and were called upon to perform a wide range of public duties, as well as presiding over council meetings. Here are two of the many duties carried out by High Street newsagent Cllr Jack Davies and his wife, Mayor and Mayoress from 1957-1959; the mayoress lays a brick at the new Friary Hall Further Education Centre in Lower Galdeford.

The Mayor and Mayoress visit east Hamlet Hospital to present a birthday cake to centenarian Mrs Bytheway from Ludford. They are watched by relatives.

The culmination of the parish church restoration campaign was a service of thanksgiving on 30 June 1959, attended by Princess Margarte. Her Royal Highness is seen here leaving the church by the west door, attended by the Bishop of Hereford (left) and by Bishop E.W. Sara (right). Bishop Sara, assistant Bishop of Hereford and Rector of Ludlow from 1945 to 1963, performed great services for the town, including his vigorous leadership of the Restoration.

The flagship of the Restoration programme was the production of John Milton's masque *Comus*, specially written for performance at Ludlow Castle in 1634. This was presented by a professional cast, assisted by local amateurs in non-speaking parts. The masque was staged in 1953, bringing the restoration programme great publicity, and was repeated in 1958 with some changes in the cast. There was a single repeat performance of the 1958 production in 1959 for Princess Margaret's visit.

In this scene from the 1958 production, *Comus* (John Westbrook) seeks to seduce the lady (Peggy Butt). They are surrounded by Comus' *crew* or *rabble*, former courtiers transformed into demi-beasts after succumbing to the temptations which the Lady, symbolising virtue, is able to resist. Members of the crew, not all shown here, were: Giles Angell, Pat Caulfield, Barbara Didlick, Daphne Evans, Walter Hillman, Anthony Ingram, Janet Lewis, Maureen Moore, Robert Rose, Ian Slater, Michael Walters, Janice Watkins, Audrey Weller, Norma Williamson, Sheila Williamson, Connie Williams.

Seven

1960-1969

In common with most of the country, living standards in this decade continued to rise, prompting the political catch phrase, 'You've never had it so good'. Nationally, this was a time of great social and cultural change, but at Ludlow innovations came slowly. The town escaped the kind of large scale development that blighted larger places such as Shrewsbury and Worcester, and many pleasing housing estates were laid out north and east of the earlier town.

Ludlow, which had a population of 6, 796 in 1961, was still small enough for individuals to have great influence. Some of these, such as Fred Reeves, Gladys Porter and Bill Price, are featured in subsequent pages. Another titan, pictured below, was Arthur Reynolds, the first chairman of Ludlow Festival.

Arthur Reynolds, MBE, was a Quaker, a man of great faith, who had served with distinction as a major in the Eighth Army. He settled in Ludlow in 1945, founding Reynolds Woodware Ltd in vacant premises at the bottom of Lower Broad Street, where high quality furniture was produced. He and his wife created the Ludlow Folk Dance Group and during the 1950s Morris Dancers were a familiar sight in south Shropshire. Arthur was very involved in the church restoration plays of the 1950s – he led the dancing peasants in *Comus* – and it was he who was the prime force in starting the Ludlow Festival in 1960, with *Midsummer Night's Dream* in the Castle and four supporting events. He was elected the festival's first chairman but tragically died in December 1960. He had, however, laid a foundation on which others quickly built. One person who saw the 1960 Festival production was James Roose-Evans, director of *Pericles* in 2000, and he thought it right to dedicate that production to Arthur's memory, writing in the programme notes: 'Belief in community ventures ran like a thread through Arthur Reynolds' life and when promoting the idea of a Ludlow Festival this was always his major argument'.

Winners of this National Competition were the members of the
LUDLOW BRITISH LEGION DARTS TEAM L-R:
Standing:
Tommy Morris   Charles Morris   Frank Hughes
Seated:
Jack Adams   Roy Nash   Joe Wait   George Hughes

Darts has been a popular game in Ludlow throughout the century, with teams being formed
from public houses and social clubs. By 1960 over 400 players were registered in the town,
competing in local leagues. Dominoes was another game organized in this way, while later in
the century there was also a league for general knowledge quiz teams. The photograph shows
the Ludlow British Legion Darts Team, winners of a national competition in 1960. All the were
men were well-known locally, especially Joe Wait the undertaker.

The new swimming pool was opened at Dinham Bridge on Sunday, 11 May 1961. The provision of this facility, much needed in the town, was a massive achievement. The total cost was £31,000, £22,000 of which was raised through a local football pool by a body known as the Ludlow Guild. This is a view across the open air pool, towards the former Castle Mill which was adopted as changing rooms. By autumn 1962 the pool had been enclosed, with large windows facing the river, and a roof supported by cruck-like beams.

A plaque outside the building was unveiled by Wilfred Packer, chief promoter of the Guild, and reads: 'This swimming bath owes its being to the Ludlow Guild and particularly to the vision and enterprise of its founder members: Roy Ashton, George M. Bellwood, George E.C. Grimmett, Winifred M. Jones, Robert T. Lloyd, Wilfred L. Packer, Violet J. Packer, Gladys M. Potter, Sidney E. Price, William Price, Edward E. Sheldon, Ronald C. Thatcher, Reginald C. Wakeman, T. Brydon Yarrow.' In the 1990s, to conform with new regulations and to provide up-to-date facilities, new swimming baths were built at Burway, as part of the South Shropshire Leisure Centre. Part of the funding came from the sale of the Dinham swimming bath to a reconstituted Ludlow Guild, who have demolished the old structure and brought the site back into public use as a riverside open space. The spirit of self-help in Ludlow lives on triumphantly.

A street scenes at the hub of the town, radiating from the eighteenth century Butter Cross. This view of the top of Broad Street is one of a number of studies of Ludlow streetscapes by a keen amateur photographer, R.T. Harris. It shows a much photographed part of Ludlow, with the upper storeys of timber-framed buildings projecting over a covered way or *piazza*. The signs can be seen of Valentines, long established family grocers, and De Grey's cafe, a popular eating place and rendezvous since it was established in the 1920s.

The western end of King Street, with the familiar over-hang of F. Bodenham Outfitters, on the left. The building next to it, castigated by the architectural historian Alec Clifton-Taylor as 'the ugliest in Ludlow', then accommodated the International Stores, a multiple grocery chain, and a small private business belonging to Eileen Gerard, selling good quality ladies' clothes.

Social and interest groups continued to proliferate; this was the cast of an Edwardian music hall type concert, which had been presented in the town hall. They were having an after-show party at the Angel Hotel. Those present included Connie Faulkner (standing far left), Don Faulkner (standing third from left), Richard Francis (standing fourth from left, later organist at St Laurence's), Yvonne Harper (standing eighth from left, manageress of the Angel Hotel), Malcolm Beagley (next to Yvonne), David Wiles (standing far right), Dolly Martin (sitting centre), Dorothy Beagley, nee Wait (sitting right of centre).

One of the groups providing companionship and social activities were the Young Wives. They were founded in the early 1950s under the auspices of the parish church but later became Ludlow Parish Wives, with a looser church affiliation. This was a group of members after an annual dinner: From left to right, standing: May Jackson, Phyllis Sadler, Elise Allerton, Betty Duce, Mable Brown, Audrey Dahn, Margaret Jones. Sitting: Peggy Carter, Connie Willliams, Gwen Barr (leader), Joyce Lovett.

Another photograph by R.T. Harris, taken in 1964 from the top of the parish church tower looking towards the Bull Ring and Upper Galdeford. It shows some of Ludlow's best known buildings, including the rear of the Bull Hotel (bottom left), the richly carved facade of the Feathers and the narrower timber-framed building to the right, later occupied by Emporos. Beyond, on the far side of Portcullis Lane, are the crowded plots of Upper Galdeford, while in the top left corner can be seen one of the town's former brick fields, with grass covering the uneven surface.

A view along Upper Galdeford, showing the Victorian Portcullis Inn on the right, with houses and a few shops beyond. On the right is the long brick range of The Ludlow *Advertiser* buildings, erected in 1913. Much of the ground floor was rented for shops but the *Advertiser* office can be seen on the right. The paper was printed at Ludlow for some years but later this operation was transferred to Stourport. The *Tizer*, especially while it was edited locally, was a popular local newspaper, well known for its support to worthy local causes.

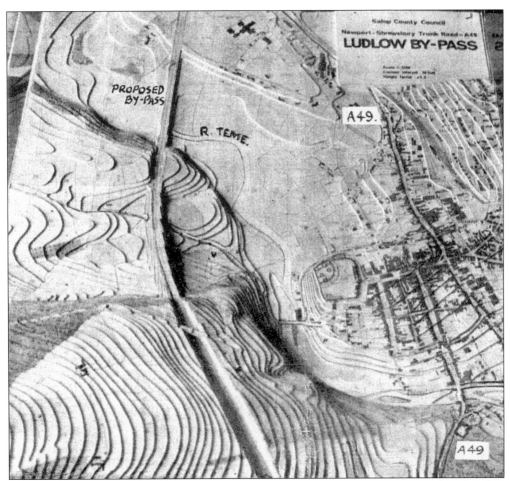

An issue of lively debate during the 1960s was the route to be taken by a proposed Ludlow by-pass. The urgent need for such a road was agreed by everyone, as the growing volume of commercial and private traffic continued to pound the town centre, causing massive congestion and shaking the foundations of historic buildings. At one public meeting the County Council's Surveyor's Department proposed a route west of the town, with a deep cutting through Whitcliffe 'so that the traffic would not be seen', but this was bitterly opposed by Ludlow people, headed by the Civic Society and the Whitcliffe commoners. In the end a route east of the town was chosen, though it involved the loss of good farm land. The by-pass eventually opened in 1977.

The mounting of a major arts festival 'by the courageous citizens of a small country town' (*Hereford Evening News*, 1962), was a bold venture which faltered badly in 1963, where there was a heavy financial loss, but then recovered to become well-established by the end of the decade. The centre-piece was a Shakespeare play in the inner bailey of the castle. The photograph shows a scene from *Richard II* in 1963. Reviewers of this and later plays noted the dramatic qualities of the castle, 'where voices bounced off the rugged walls... like balls from a squash court'. The production itself, however, was criticised in *The Birmingham Post* as 'rather stark, unpageant-like, astringent.'

Measure for Measure in 1967, was more favourably received. *The Times* reported that 'Joan Knight's production is fluent and holds the attention well'. The distinctive ethos of Ludlow Festival was noted by many visitors, as in 1969 at a production of *Romeo and Juliet*, when, 'the old hands weighed down with equipment – blankets, cushions and thermos flasks – were likened to 'the British about to set off on Safari'.

This photograph records a sad event – the last meeting of Ludlow Borough Council in 1967. As a result of the 1958 Local Government Act, Ludlow, with many other small historic towns, now became a rural borough with reduced powers, many of its functions being transferred to Ludlow Rural District Council at Stone House. Many guests, including former mayors, had crowded into the Town Hall Council Chamber for the occasion. The Mayor, Cllr W. Price, presides, with the deputy Mayor, Cllr E. Sheldon, on his right, and the town clerk, JP Mallony, on his left. The speaker, on her feet, is Cllr Gladys Potter.

This was the Ludlow Library Consultative Committee, which was set up under the auspices of Shropshire County Council to liase with local people on library matters. The meeting was chaired by Fred Reeves, a history master at Ludlow Grammar School from 1928-1965 and a tireless worker for conservation and cultural causes in Ludlow. When Fred died in 1980, an obituary notice said of him: 'If there is a committee in heaven, Fred will be on it, probably as chairman, almost certainly puffing his pipe.'

Buying and selling at the covered market in Ludlow Town hall. The Town Hall stood in the middle of Castle Street, which had been the site of the town's market since the twelfth century or earlier, though the livestock market moved elsewhere after 1860. The stallholder, on the right, was Dorothy Carter selling fruit and vegetables; she still lives in Ludlow. These photographic studies are early works by Paul Hill, the son of a Ludlow based Inspector of Police and an old boy of Ludlow Grammar School. He left journalism to become a professional photographer. He is now Professor of Photography at De Montfort University, Leicester, and in 1994 was awarded the MBE for services to photography.

An employee leaves the Picture House after a late showing. The Picture House, the older and less well furbished of Ludlow's two cinemas, was affectionately known as 'the flea pit', but the films shown here in the post-war years brought great pleasure to many. The cinema was especially popular with children on Saturday mornings.

Another photographic study by Paul Hill, showing two unidentified ladies looking through one of the windows of the premises of Chipps of Ludlow, furniture dealers. The building is now used by Sykes and Co. Accountants.

Another evocative study by Paul Hill. Old men, not among Ludlow's most prosperous citizens, echo the vertical lines of the Butter Cross, itself showing symptoms of decay. Throughout the century senior citizens have gathered at or near this place, to gossip and to watch the world go by.

Eight
1970-1979

The 1970s saw the continued outward growth of Ludlow, as new private housing estates were laid out, enlarged and consolidated. Later pictures in this chapter show some of the town's oldest traditions – the May Fair, races at Bromfield, and a continuing wide range of leisure activities. There are a number of street scenes, and a glimpse of McConnels – representatives of the town's widening industrial base. People of many ages are portrayed, from the Brownies on p. 92 to one of the town's best known older citizens, Manny Weaver, on p. 102.

Charlton Rise off Sheet Road, with the field known as Gallow's Bank to the left. The use of this open land, once a place of public execution, became a subject of great debate in later years. However at the end of the twentieth century its designation as a millennium green was confirmed.

The second Ludlow pack of Brownies, at Craven Arms on St George's Day, 1970, when they attended a church service and gathered afterwards with other packs for Brownie Revels. The Brownies were one of several uniformed organizations in the town. The Brown Owl (back left) was Jenny Vaughan who has had a career of outstanding public service in Ludlow over many years. The Brownies were, from left to right, back row: Linda Small, -?-, Susan Webster (not yet in uniform), Jackie Blackburn, Cheryl Pritchard, Zoe Beeching, Sally Owen, Dawn Watkins (not yet in uniform), Gillian Phelps, Donita Lucas, Corrine Haynes, Elizabeth Boundford, Charlotte Preece. Front row: Christina Phelps, Cheryl Sanders, -?-, Mandy Marsh, Sandra Hicks.

Older girls are here participating in the crowning of Miss Ludlow, an event organized by Festive Ludlow. This is Judith Perry, the 1976 Miss Ludlow, with her attendants Wendy Brown (left) and Wendy Magrail (right). She is being crowned by the retiring Miss Ludlow, Rachel Thomas.

One of the oldest and most enduringly popular Ludlow events is the May Fair. This began as a commercial fair, held on the feast of St Philip and St James (1 May) and on the days either side. As livestock markets were held more regularly, most fairs lapsed in the nineteenth century, but the May Fair survived, first for the hiring of servants, then for pleasure. 'The Gallopers' in Castle Square in 1972 can be seen, with a glimpse of the dodgems to the left. These and similar 'big rides' were owned by well-known 'show business' families, first the Hills, then the Wynns, who contracted with other showmen, such as the Stokes brothers, to provide supporting stalls and entertainments.

This photograph taken by Gareth Thomas shows the Orbiter and the helter-skelter in Upper Mill Street, with the rotating lights of the Orbiter weaving patterns of light. Candles and gas lamps have long been evocative features of night-time fairgrounds; electricity now allows extravaganzas of light to be created.

Races on the Old Field at Bromfield maintained their popularity throughout the twentieth century, with five meetings a year, lasting two days, during the 1970s. This is the Hunters' Chase on 1 March 1972, with the horses taking the water jump in front of the Grand Stand. The races provided a gathering point for landowners, farmers and others, some of them local, others from further afield.

A different kind of race was that organized as part of Ludlow's water carnival, held on the River Teme in 1975. The prize for the most novel craft was won by Dale Turkeys from Caynham, who entered this water-borne steam engine, with a crew of six to wield the paddles.

A large crowd gathered in Castle Square in 1973 to watch the completion of a charity walk by Derek Dougan, the popular Wolverhampton professional footballer. Here Amos Bradley of Ludlow is pictured carrying his brother Tony over the finishing line, to the great entertainment of the crowd as they wait for Dougan and his party to arrive. The Bradley brothers belonged to a large Ludlow family one of whom, Rosemary Jones, was Mayor in 1999-2000.

The first XI of Ludlow and South Shropshire Cricket Club, photographed in front of the pavilion at Burway at the end of 1974 season. The Hern brothers in the front row were part of Ludlow Cricketing dynasty, with their father Sidney and brother Robert also playing for the club. From left to right, standing: Michael Burgoyne, Hugh Morgan, John Kemp, Terry Healy, Richard Stephens, Robin Freeman, Clive Edwards, Bert Nason (umpire). Sitting: Tony Hern, Eric Marsh, Jim Hern, (captain), Alan Cade.

A float from the 1976 Carnival, organized by Festive Ludlow. It was presented by pupils of Ludlow Stage School and was one of a number of dancing ventures promoted by Brenda and Owen Dahl. They are posing as Alexander's Rag Time Band on a lorry of Rickards and Co., long established ironmongers. From left to right, on the lorry: Deborah Cade, Joanna Peachey, Ian Dahl (Uncle Sam), Michelle James, Andrea Cade, Sarah Grundey, Judith Jennings, Jane Evans. Walking, left hand column: Paula Beadles, Julia Honeyfield, Helen Tomkins, Juliet Klein, Susan Bird. Walking, right hand column: Karen Morris, Frances Thomas, Tania Morris, Catherine Winrow, Joanna Banks. Standing beside the open window is Phil Hamer, driver of the lorry.

F.W. McConnel, Ltd, was one of Ludlow's largest employers, making hedge cutters and other kinds of agricultural machinery at their factory in Weeping Cross Lane which had been built as a food store during the Second World War. The picture shows the complete engineering department. It was taken in June 1975, when McConnels won the Royal Agricultural Society of England's gold medal for innovating hydraulically powered agricultural machinery. From left to right: Martin Fisher, Bill Norton, (design director), Graham Berlin, George Watt, Bill Jones (consultant), John Bishop, Fritz Barrels, George Perks, Audrey Froggatt, Peter Cooper, Ian Robertson, Ceri Morgan (Development and Prototype Supervisor), David Froggatt (superintendent technical publications), Mike Bowen, Howard Gregory, Stephen Weake, Glyn 'Tiger' Jones, John Hughes (chief draughtsman), Len Eyles, David Eaglestone, Gerald Wheelwright, Les Brown, Russell Jones.

Bill Norton receiving the gold medal from His Royal Highness the Prince of Wales at the Royal Show at Stoneleigh in Warwickshire.

Old Street, once part of an ancient track-way along the Welsh border, was very rarely as devoid of traffic as in this photograph, taken in 1976. The buildings on the right were formerly the Golden Lion Inn, the upper part of which was adopted as a library – for which purpose the premises were grossly unsuitable. Further down can be seen the early seventeenth century Preacher's house and beyond Old Street garage, later replaced by Ashford Mews, a housing complex. As from most places in Ludlow, green fields and trees can be seen in the distance.

Part of Temeside, with the entrance to St John's Lane (once Frog Lane) on the left, and part of the Old Street mill on the right. The large hoarding was sited to catch the attention of motorists travelling between Ludford Bridge and the bottom of Old Street. The hoarding, the house behind it and the gardens beyond were later replaced by the South Shropshire District Council housing complex known as Lower Fee.

A production of Noel Coward's classic comedy, *Hay Feaver* in 1975 by Ludlow Amateur Dramatic Society. There has been a series of such groups in Ludlow during the twentieth century, but the LADS, founded in the early 1970s and still operating in 2000, has been the longest-lasting. From left to right: Jan Rose (director), Wendy Hirons, Pam Reece, Connie Williams, Keith Bridgewater, Pat Calendar, Elisabeth Masters, John Corfield, Peter Wagstaffe.

A children's play, *Where the Rainbow Ends*, also directed by Jan Rose, was presented in January 1976. Members of the cast included Jeremy Hardwick (St George), Nicholas Coote (the Dragon King), Paddy Harwick, Philipa Rose, Jeremy Rose, Linda Calendar and Adam Wickers.

It was a happy coincidence that a royal visit to Ludlow occurred in 1977, the year when the nation celebrated the twenty-fifth anniversary of the reign of Queen Elizabeth II. Princess Alexandra can be seen here greeting elderly and disabled people in Post Office Square on the evening of Saturday, 9 July, on her way to watch the Ludlow Festival performance of *Henry V* in the castle. It was reported in *The Ludlow Advertiser* that, 'People in their hundreds turned out to wave and cheer along the processional way.'

One of the many street parties which took place in Ludlow to celebrate the Silver Jubilee. This one was at Oldgate Fee, where a new council estate had been built a few years previously to replace older houses, with the distinctive feature of lock-up garages below some of the terraces. Among the standing adults are: Harry Glaze (at the rear, drinking tea), Maizie Cadwallader, Helen Hill, Geraldine Griffiths, Margaret McGarrity, Mary Williams, Lorraine Didlick, Jean Candy, Sue Candy, Kay Didlick, Jan Monteith, Jan Wooton, the Mayor and Mayoress of Ludlow (councillor and Mrs Bateman), Douglas Jacks, Thirza Sibbons, Marjorie Weaver, Rita Gough. The children, standing or sitting at the front, include: Beverley Cox, Katrina Cox, Nicky Goldthorpe, Emma Gough, Louise Green, Sharon Hill, Wendy Marston, Shelly McGainty, Andrew McNinch, Sean McNinch, Andrien Monteith, Nicholas Monteith, Paula Mytton, Glynn Price, Andrew Sibbons, Philip Sibbons, Toni Sibbons, Andrew Webster, Anthony Wootton.

As illustrated by this photograph of High Street, taken by R.T. Harris in 1978, the historic townscapes of today have resulted from a long process of development. Here medieval encroachment and infilling, within the wide market place laid out by the Normans, has produced a crowded town centre of narrow streets and awkward corners. The narrow shops on the left, once called Shoemakers Row, reflect the proportions of medieval stalls or *selda* arranged in a line down the middle of the once much wider High Street. Ahead the vista is closed by the early fifteenth century façade of Bodenhams, the uppermost of a series of properties pushing into the market place from Broad Street, as the burgesses of the day sought the most advantageous trading positions. Beyond, the narrow defile twists into King Street, where delivery vans are causing congestion in the part of the town once known as Drapers Row.

One of the strongest groups in Ludlow over many years was the Townswomen's Guild, pictured here at their annual dinner on 5 December 1979. The branch was opened in 1933, becoming part of the Shropshire and mid-Wales Federation of Townswomen's Guilds. The officers on the top table, from left to right: Doris Faraday (secretary), Marie Nicholas (treasurer), Minnie Price (vice-president), Effie Judd (president), Ellen Mackenzie (chairman), Mrs Alice Price-Wood (vice-president), Mary Cooper (vice-chairman). Other members behind: Mary Lloyd, -?-, Crundell, -?-, -?-, ? Jayne, -?-, Lorne Britt, Dorothy Mundy, -?-, Olive MacVicar, Betty Goff, Pat Powers, ? Dwight, Mary North, Joan Trotman, Audrey Pinches, Gladys Dyer, Elisabeth Holt, Connie Faulkner, Doris Price, Cissie Edwards, Dorothy Brazier, -?-, Evelyn Whysall, Betty Stones, -?-, Betty Stephens, Roma Beard, Winnie Faulkner.

Someone from a different sector of Ludlow's society was 'Manny' Weaver, a well-known personality seen here collecting wood from Whitcliffe with his donkey and cart.

Nine

1980-1989

Most of the ensuing pictures illustrate a town of continuing beauty and charm, with a remarkably successful festival and many signs of community endeavour and success. But beneath the surface, as in many other towns, this was a time of re-alignment, and sometimes a time of turmoil. Nationally, it was decade of lively and often passionate politics with outbreaks of civil strife over the poll tax, the miners' strike and financial cuts. This had its echoes in Ludlow, where great local feeling was aroused over proposals to abolish the maternity unit, and later, one of the wards at Ludlow hospital. There was concern too about the conditions of some of the town's council housing, and at related social issues, and many pleaded for better facilities for young people. However, for many the most regrettable events of the decade were the demolition in 1986 of the Town Hall and the Clifton cinema.

The reorganization of local government had left the town council with greatly reduced powers and responsibilities, but concern about the issues listed above brought a wave of new members onto the council in 1987, several of whom were determined and articulate. Within a few years the council had resumed some of its traditional responsibilities, including the street market and cemetery, and was deeply involved, along with other local bodies, in the campaign to refurbish the Assembly Rooms to meet community facilities in lieu of those lost in 1986.

The conservation of the historic environment was another major social concern and in this area the planning department of SSDC, in spite of some unfortunate decisions earlier in the decade, gave a purposeful lead, prompted by Ludlow Civic Society and other amenity groups. A series of local plans, the designation of a Ludlow conservation area and the listing of more Ludlow buildings, in the 1980s and 1990s, went a long way towards safe-guarding the town centre though the sanctity of surrounding countryside was often threatened and sometimes breached.

This photograph of Ludlow on a winter's morning late in 1985 shows the early sunlight picking up a number of buildings in the town centre, including the Town Hall.

Between 1955 and 1981 a vast collection of fossils, specimens and artefacts was gathered in the room over the Butter Cross. Beginning with articles which had survived from the Victorian museum in the Assembly Rooms, a remarkable set of exhibits was lovingly assembled and presented by John Norton of Bromfield, a professional auctioneer, who had been, since childhood, an enthusiast for geology, wildlife and history. John Norton is showing exhibits to school children and their teacher. There were three such groups who went to the museum during these years, lured by Johns' dedication and reputation. In 1976 he was awarded the MBE for 'services to museums.'

A section of the museum, with exhibits of various kinds in display cabinets. When Ian Nairn, the architectural critic visited Ludlow in 1972 he wrote, 'A local museum that is the best I've seen in Britain, all crammed in and exciting. You begin with Victorian bygones and end up hooked on geology and the Crested Grebe.'

The picture shows a presentation to Nancy Philips, who had been headmistress of St Laurence's Church of England Infants School, once called the National, since 1964. It was made by prebendary Ray Morrison, rector of Ludlow and chairman of the governors, and Dr Martin Speight, Mayor of Ludlow who also had children at the school.

The presentation of awards to the cadets of St John's Ambulance Brigade. From left to right, standing: Joanna Hughes, Sarah Entecott, Sara Hawkes, Jenny Senior, Sadie Hughes, Ann Marie Price, Rachel Smallman, Stacy Rogers, Emma Meak, Helen Dunn, Sarah Bun, Sarah Meak, Emma Weir, Christine Little, Amy Pritchard, Robert Gissop, Linda Entecott, Richard Mellings, Pat Boreman, Ian Ridgeway, Martin Brain, Rose Charlton, Judy Deakin, Wendy Smallman, Mabel Tristram, Alec Peachy, Lady Plymouth, Lady Forester. Back row: Sharon ?, -?-, -?-, Danielle ?, Catherine Adams, Karen Whitehouse, Sarah Tate. Third row: Helen Whitehouse, Lucy Holiday, Elsie Thomas, Katie Bryant. Second row: Jenny Dunn, Sonia Turner, Kelly Powell, Louise Edwards, Emma Meredith, Katherine Farnham, -?-, Amy Barker. Front row: Claire Thomas, Linsey Geary, Tracy Nicholas, Sarah Grant, Julie Hiles, Katie Bryan, Kirsty White.

Since the Ludlow Festival began in 1960, the performance of a Shakespearian play in the inner bailey of the castle has been the major event of Ludlow Festival, though supported by a rich programme of concerts, exhibitions, country house evenings and other events. This view shows David Kelsey's 1981 production of *As you Like It*, described in the programme notes as 'this evergreen popular Elizabethan comedy.'

106

This production was well received. The *Hereford Times* reviewer described it as 'a light mixture of poetry and pantomime'. *The Birmingham Post* reviewer considered Nyree Dawn-Porter as 'one of the most graceful Rosalinds I have seen', while of Nicholas Smith's portrayal of Jacques he reported; 'rarely have I heard the seven ages of man handled so beautifully since Max Adrian's days at Stratford.' Much of the festival's success is due to the talents and dedication of members of the Festival Council and of a great army of helpers. A particular strength has been the art work, which has reached high standards in the publicity papers designed for many years by Polly Hamilton, and in the covers of the festival programme, one of which, that for 1981 by Valerie Alexander, is illustrated here.

A quiet scene in Ludlow, outside Reg Martin and Sons, one of several family butchers in the town at this time. Most of these butchers had links with Welsh border farms and meat came directly to them from local slaughter-houses. The shop occupies part of a much larger building, which was the Red Lion Inn in the eighteenth century. The brick elevation masks an earlier timber frame, going back to the sixteenth century, when these were the premises of Thomas Blashfield, the town's leading clothier.

Behind its elegant street frontages and high walls, Ludlow has many fine gardens occupying the rear parts of one or more burgage plots. This aerial photograph reveals such gardens on the eastern side of Broad Street and off Brand Lane. One of the largest is that behind No. 27 Broad Street (on the far right) which has been amalgamated with that of a property in Brand Lane. This huge area, once owned by the Charltons of Ludford and from 1764 by Somerset Davies, a successful lawyer, has a delightful gazebo, visible near the top of the picture, beside the large tree.

From 1990 a number of the 'secret gardens' of Ludlow, by kind agreement of their owners, have been open to the public for one afternoon in mid-summer, in order to raise funds for Ludlow Assembly Rooms. This has become a popular annual event, attracting large crowds each year. The picture shows such an open garden at Maryvale, a long property running back from Mill Street between the brick wall against Camp Lane on the left and the thirteenth century town wall on the right.

The presentation of Prometheus by Ludlow School at the finals of the Barclays Youth Music Theatre Awards at the Royal Albert Hall, London, in 1985. The school came First, one of a series of remarkable successes in national competitions gained by the school at this time. Ludlow School is a comprehensive which took its first all ability entry in 1977, occupying the buildings of the former Secondary Modern School at Burway.

LUDLOW SCHOOL CHOIR
Conductor: *Anthony Knight*
Prometheus   *Anthony Knight*
                              Libretto: Joanna
                              Knight

Ludlow School is a rural comprehensive of just over 1,000 pupils with a catchment area of over 400 square miles. Music plays an important part in the school curriculum with great emphasis being placed on creative work within the classroom.

The school first entered the National Festival in 1983. Since then the school band has performed in the Festival Hall and the senior choir has received the Outstanding Performance Award for the last two years in the Voices in Concert section. The previous highlight was last year's performance by the choir of 'The Willow Pattern' in the Schools Prom. The choir has grown since last year and now numbers 55 pupils, some of whom have never visited London before, let alone performed in the Royal Albert Hall.

Prometheus — *Anthony Knight*

Prometheus is a music drama specially written for the choir's entry in this year's National Festival of Music for Youth. Told through a combination of choir,

instrumentalists and movement, the work is a contemporary version of ancient Greek legends surrounding the figure of Prometheus.

We see his creation of mankind, his stealing of fire to give man warmth and his subsequent punishment by the Gods. Doomed to die a thousand deaths, he is powerless to prevent mankind's corruption. On the wind his voice cries out in pain but the Gods reject him.

LUDLOW SCHOOL CHOIR
Conductor: *Anthony Knight*
Make up & costume: *Sheila Rose, Geraldine Rose, Julia Honeyfield*
Age range of performers: *13–17 years*

Choir	Instrumentalists
Christine Morgan	Bruce Waite
Judith O'Donovan	Richard Griffiths
Jo Basten	Isabel Kydd
Margaret Taylor	Rosalind Taylor
Kim Nicholas	Sarah Ayres
Erica Waite	Katie Moses
Kim Edwards	Julie Cordingley
Suzanne Collette	Sarah Holland
Helen Bews	Debbie Venables
Ruth Starns	Anne Watkins
Sharron Jackson	
Charlotte Evans	**Movement**
Catherine Ewins	Denis Jones
Joanne Benton	Eaun McPherson
Rebecca Tudge	Peter Crouch
Elizabeth Precious	Beverley Reid
Alison Briant	Alice Hooton
Jane Lilley	Alison Kydd
Maddy Speed	Hannah Tudge
Lynne Watkins	Katie Mountford
Vickie Sinclair	Joanne Ellis
Penny Lovatt	
Carol Wilding	
Debbie Smallman	
Claire Morris	
Helen Smallwood	
Sarah Cooke	
Nicola Denton	
Anna Wainwright	
Clare Powell	
Leo Dodd	
Lara Furniss	
Emma Wise	

Programme for Prometheus, 1985.

1986 was a calamitous year for Ludlow, with the demolition, for different reasons, of the Town Hall and Clifton Cinema. The demolition of the Town Hall by South Shropshire District Council, who had taken responsibility for it from Ludlow Town Council in 1974, was arguably the saddest Ludlow event of the century. The building had been deteriorating for some years, but had action been taken after a surveyor's report received in 1981, it could have been saved. The covered market, the spacious hall above and the fine council chamber – visible through the broken bay window on the main photograph – were valued public amenities, which had been provided, with civic pride, less than a hundred years previously.

The front of the Clifton Cinema, with Miss Jones, who operated the box office for many years. Opened in 1938, the cinema closed in the 1970s and became a bingo hall, but a vociferous local group felt it should be preserved for its architectural qualities and as a public amenity. However it was demolished to make way for a large sheltered housing complex called Clifton Court. Though many estimable people now have comfortable accommodation there, the loss of the cinema is still widely regretted.

This beautiful composition by Gareth Thomas shows Ludlow Castle on its natural defensive site above the River Teme, with the great hall and its windows just to the right of centre. With infinite patience the photographer has succeeded in portraying a swimming coot at the central point in his picture. This is an uncanny echo of a painting nearly two hundred years earlier, when the romantic landscape painter, J.M.W. Turner, shows a duck in a similar position in one of his three known paintings of Ludlow Castle.

This bird's eye view takes in the roofscapes of Lower Broad Street. When Prince Charles visited Ludlow in 1994 he spoke of, 'the varied yet harmonious roofscapes of the town' as one of its most enjoyable features. The photograph also shows the medieval Ludford Bridge, with its triangular breakers – the historic entrance to Ludlow from the south, crossing the River Teme. Beyond is the core of the village of Ludford, grouped around the parish church of St Giles, beyond which can be seen parts of Ludford House, with its spacious grounds. This is the largest house in the immediate vicinity of Ludlow, having evolved over many centuries from a medieval leper hospital.

Dinham can be seen in the foreground, with some of the buildings on Mill Street behind. Dinham is a distinctive part of Ludlow, indeed some historians believe that it is the oldest part of the town. At the core is a triangular piece of ground, in the middle of which can be seen St Thomas's chapel. This is a late Norman building, built shortly after the murder of Thomas Beckett in 1172, though the roof, the cupola and the traceried window date from the eighteenth century. This has always been a residential area, with a number of large dwellings, some of which can be seen here. There are also some smaller dwellings such as the timber-framed cottage to the right of the chapel.

Ten

1990-2000

The pace of change quickened in the 1990s. Some of the schemes conceived or started in the late 1980s came to triumphant conclusions: a new building for St Laurence's Infants' School, the Assembly Rooms, the leisure centre at Burway, and the Rockspring Centre on the Sandpits Estate. The town's outward growth continued, with new estates off Sheet road, off Fishmore Road and at Burway. A number of conservation schemes began or were rejuvenated, often bringing ad hoc trusts into being, including the Weirs Trust to whom this book is dedicated.

Ludlow's reputation as a place to live in and to visit was enhanced. People retiring to Ludlow included many who had achieved great things in earlier careers – and some of these made their talents available to their adoptive town. On 29 April 1999, the front cover of Country Life carried these remarkable headlines: 'Fanfare For Ludlow. Why has it become the town where everybody would like to live?' Some of this reputation was ascribed to the town's three Michelin Star restaurants, a higher number than anywhere outside London.

Many retired people stressed the attractiveness of a small community, the town's rural setting, the fine scenery and buildings. However, not everyone saw life in Ludlow as an idyll. In spite of the new leisure centre, some felt that the needs of the young were still not adequately catered for. Poverty, deprivation and other social ills lurked in parts of the town. Planning issues brought fierce debate, especially over the movement of the livestock market to a site on Overton Road and at the prospect of another supermarket. Traffic control and management remained serious issues but by 2000 no real solutions had been found, in spite of the start in that year of a much modified town enhancement scheme in Castle Square.

A mechanical digger begins work in 1990 on the new site for St Laurence's Infants' School, between Holdgate Fee and Friar's Walk. There were many building schemes during these years.

Ludlow Photographic Club, formerly the Camera Club, was first founded in 1897, perhaps inspired by visits to the town in 1895 and 1896 of Henry Peach Robinson, a photographic artist of national standing who had been born and educated in Ludlow. The first secretary was J.H. Williams, town clerk, with J.H. Suttle, chemist and supplier of photographic materials, and J.E. Pughe, borough surveyor, among the first members. In common with the original club, the highlight of the year's programmes is the annual exhibition. Here, such an exhibition is being mounted in the Barbara Dyer Room at Ludlow College. On the left Anthony Roberts, Esther Barton and Gareth Thomas – all past chairmen – are assessing a print prior to hanging. On the right is Karen Birch, a regular contributor. The club thrives today and has readily embraced the new digital technology which promises to revolutionise photography in the twenty-first century.

Members of Ludlow Civic Society outside the Assembly Rooms at Pitville, Cheltenham, on their way back from a residential historical and architectural weekend at Bath University, led by David Lloyd. Against a column in the back row, with an open necked shirt, is Stephen Dornan, a Ludlow solicitor with a remarkable knowledge of buildings, who was a dedicated and effective chairman of the society from 1990-1996. The Civic Society has had a substantial impact on public affairs in Ludlow since its inception in 1954.

Hosyer's Almshouse, an elegant mid-eighteenth century building in College Street, overlooking St Laurence's churchyard. The endowment was made in the fifteenth century by John Hosyer, a rich Ludlow merchant. There were originally thirty-three chambers for elderly persons, but in recent years these have been transformed into fifteen flats, some for single people, others for married couples.

One of the residents, Miss Evelyn Nash, in her living room at the Almshouses, with the living-in-warden, Mrs Linda Bissell. This photograph was taken in June 1993, a few weeks before a visit by his Royal Highness Prince Charles, Patron of the Almshouses Association.

In an age of supermarkets and sliced bread, 'we bake our own bread' is the proud boast of S.C. Price and Sons, family bakers and confectioners of No. 7 Castle Street. These photographs were taken in 1993 to mark the fiftieth anniversary of the acquisition of the business by Sidney Price from Davies and Brown, previous bakers on the premises. Five of the children of Sidney and Martha Price were partners in the business in 1993. This shows the bakery in Quality Square, with trays of newly baked bread loaves freshly taken from the ovens. These were carried on wheeled trolleys across Caste Square to the shop – a regular Ludlow spectacle. From left to right: Gerald Price, Ivor Barnett.; Geoffrey Price (husband of Sheila Price), Trevor Price.

The staff in the shop, standing behind the counter: From left to right, back row: Alex Gifford, Diane Jackson (temporary assistant), Deborah Cook (daughter of Sheila Barnett), Peter Cook (husband of Deborah). Front row: Sheila Barnett (nee Price), Edna Lewis (nee Price), Jenny Price (wife of Gerald).

For some years at the end of the century Festive Ludlow swathed the town centre with coloured Christmas lights, using funds raised during the preceding year. Here Upper Broad Street is seen glittering with reflections from wet road surfaces, and pools of light in shop windows. The lights, enjoyed by people of all ages, are a throw back to pagan mid-winter festivals, when bonfires blazed and candles were lit to lighten the seasonal gloom. They also proclaim the joy of a Christian Christmas, which celebrates the birth of Christ – 'Christ the Light of the World'.

Members of the Festive Ludlow Committee, who led the organization of an annual carnival and other community events during the last quarter of the century. From left to right: Jack Reece, Jenny Vaughan, Harry Peachy, Ron Miles, Martin Owen.

This remarkable photograph, of hoar frost on Whitcliffe, was taken by Gareth Thomas just after dawn on Christmas Eve 1995. It is a view of Ludlow that few people have seen, for the hoar frost, thick on trees and bushes in all directions, the result of dense, freezing fog, is quickly melted by the rising sun. Faced with such a transitory scene, the observer bows before the power of nature, and perhaps recalls Psalm 147, v.15-17:

He sendeth forth his commandment upon the earth: his word runneth very swiftly.
He giveth snow like wool: he scattereth his hoarforst like ashes.
He casteth forth his ice like morsels; who can stand before his cold?

The livestock market in progress, operated for much of the century by McCartneys, Auctioneers and Surveyors on the site off Corve Street and Station Drive. Since the twelfth century the market has been 'the lifeblood of the town', Ludlow being a centre for the buying and selling of the agricultural produce of the adjoining rural area. In the cattle pens on the far left is Tom Harper, drover, and on the far right is Roger Jones, clerk. From left to right, back row: Reg Gayther, Gary Hamer, Nicola Paddock, Phil Paddock, Malcolm Powell, Phil Amphlett, Clive Rhodes (auctioneer in white coat), John Owen, Veronica Edwards. Middle row: John Roberts, John Whiteman, Ivor Jones, Norman Jones (haulage contractor), Colin Davies, Peter Seabury, Les Norwood. Front row: Glynn Powell, David Evans.

One of the great achievements of Ludlow in the 1990s was the building of a spacious leisure centre at Burway, to be used jointly by Ludlow School and the wider community. Part of the centre can be seen on the left. Later, a fine swimming pool with ancillary facilities was added, as shown on the right of the photograph. The project was masterminded by South Shropshire District Council and Ludlow School, with Shropshire County Council and other organizations providing the capital, some of it raised by selling part of the very large school field for an edge of town housing development.

The inside of the swimming pool, which is used all day, nearly every day of the year. With these facilities added to others that have been available throughout the century – the cricket field at Burway, the rugby pitches at Linney, the football stadium at Riddings Road, the fine golf course at Bromfield and a number of tennis and bowls clubs, Ludlow, for a small country town, is very well provided with opportunities for sport and physical recreation, though new facilities for soccer are urgently needed.

The Badgers, the youngest branch of the St Johns' Ambulance Brigade, and some junior cadets entered Ludlow Carnival as 'One Hundred and One Dalmatians'. They are seen rounding the corner from Lower Galdeford just in front of Somerfield supermarket. The Dalmatians are being led into their doom by the evil Cruella DeVil, impersonated by Diana Dunn. On the far left is Linda Entecott as the family nurse, while lurking at the back is David Pugh, a sinister dog-catcher. Some of the Dalmatians were: Philip Watson Jones, Claire Rogers, Hayley Dubberley, Michelle Griffiths, Julie Alderson, Claire Ellis, Adam Lloyd, Kerry Gordon, Luke Fallows, Amanda Jones, Wendy Price, Stacey Rogers, Catherine Farnham, Gareth Dunn, Kate Salmon and Emma Lloyd. The people walking in front are Sadie Handley and Dione Handley, with Dione carrying the flag.

An important new facility in the Sandpits Avenue area, the town's largest former council housing estate, was the Rockspring Centre, which contains the Baptist church, relocated from its earlier site in Rock Lane – as well as a number of community facilities. The centre has become a focal point for local life, one mother recently calling it 'a lifeline', another saying, 'I could never have got through the summer without it'.

Alan Poulton (left), the dynamic chairman of the Friends of Whitcliffe Common, and the Earl of Plymouth, the owner of the land, are here unveiling a Toposcope, on what was sadly a very wet day. The Toposcope had been provided by the Friends to give information about the history and wildlife of the common, and to identify landmarks. Those present included, on the far right, the Revd D. Brian Curnew, Rector of Ludlow, by whom the Toposcope was blessed, and Owen Elias, Mayor of Ludlow 1995-1997. The inset shows two timber hauliers from West Yorkshire and their horse Bluebell, who had been employed by the Friends to clear overgrown trees from steeply sloping parts of the common.

An aerial view of the Assembly Rooms and the original Ludlow Museum, which had opened in 1840 after funding by voluntary subscription. After diverse uses for much of the twentieth century, the complex was refurbished and enhanced by voluntary effort from 1988, led by Ludlow and district Community Association and Ludlow Town Council. Over £400,000 was raised by 1991 and a National Lottery grant of £1,200,00 was secured in 1996. With annual attendance now over 100,000 and an employed staff of about 15 people, supported by more than 70 volunteers, the venture has been an outstanding success. One visitor observed, 'There's nothing like this in Stratford!'

The tower of St Laurence's parish church is floodlit through Ludlow Festival fortnight, as it is on many other occasions during the year. Here the steady glow of the tower – a great candle in the night – is joined momentarily by the sparkling of a fountain of light, as a mighty firework explodes against the darkness – part of a display at the end of Ludlow Festival. Ludlow Festival has been a great success story, bringing pleasure to tens of thousands of people over its forty seasons in the twentieth century. As a member of the British Arts Festival Association, its artistic reputation is high. The economic benefits to Ludlow have been immense, with local hotels and eating places packed during Festival Fortnight. A reviewer wrote in *The Lady* in 1980: 'The whole town, with its elegant architecture and rushing river, is *en fete*, warm and welcoming in a pleasingly old fashioned way'. This is a photograph by Gareth Thomas, taken from a field above Whitcliffe, using a time exposure of five seconds.

124

As at all festivals, particular habits and traditions have developed. Among them was picnicking in the outer bailey before a Festival event. This picture was taken on the last night of the Ludlow Festival in 1998, before the final concert by *The Royal Family* and *The Counterfeit Stones*.

The ecstatic faces of Ludlow's promenaders as *The Royal Family* move into their final number testifies to the pleasure, not always shown so exuberantly, which the festival brings to its audiences.

A popular event each September in the late 1990s has been the Ludlow Food and Drink Festival, a highlight of which is a 'best sausage' competition. The picture shows Chris Carter, one of the town's best known butchers, holding up one of his entries. The number of independent small businesses in the food trade is often noted and is commonly given as one of the reasons for Ludlow's high culinary reputation. In 1999 the town had three Michelin restaurants, causing it to be known as 'the gastronomic capital of the countryside'.

This photograph was taken on Sunday 17 October 1999, after a service of Thanksgiving to mark the 800th anniversary of the first rebuilding of St Laurence's parish church in 1199. From left to right: Pat Perry (church warden), Mrs Percy, Mr A.E. Percy (Her Majesty's Lord Lieutenant for Shropshire), The Rt Revd John Oliver Bishop of Hereford, Revd Brian Curnew (Rector of Ludlow), Nick Deakin (verger), The Earl of Plymouth (Patron of the Living), The Countess of Plymouth, David Lloyd (church warden).

The clearance of the former livestock market site in order to develop it as a Tesco supermarket (taken a few days after the previous photograph). The diggers, excavators and tippers transformed the site within a few days.

This magnificent picture was taken at eight o'clock on 1 January 2000. The photographer, Gareth Thomas, was alone on Whitcliffe, except for another well-known Ludlovian, Denis Nash, who was walking his dog – and enjoying the serenity of the morning. Most Ludlow residents were still asleep, many of them after seeing in the new millennium just a few hours previously. This shot records the rising sun illuminating the east facing walls of Ludlow Castle, as it often does in the early morning. Much rarer is the density of the valley mist, thickened, it is suggested, by smoke lingering from the bonfires and fireworks of celebrations the night before. It was the kind of scene that inspired Housman, though then it was the smoke of coal fires that mingled with the river vapours:

When smoke stood up from Ludlow
And mist blew off from Teme...